U.S.S. Seawolf

U.S.S. Seawolf: Submarine Raider of the Pacific

By

Gerold Frank, James D. Horan, J. M. Eckberg

Military Classics
2017

U.S.S. *Seawolf: Submarine Raider of the Pacific* by Gerold Frank, James D. Horan, J. M. Eckberg. First published in 1945. This edition published by Military Classics, 2017. All rights reserved.

Military Classics Publishing,
Los Angeles, CA.

First Printing: 2017.

ISBN 978-1-387-12101-4.

Contents

Foreword

I FEEL mighty proud to be honored by an association with submarines even as remote as writing the foreword for this real human interest story which recounts the thrilling performances of the U.S.S. *Seawolf*—one of the outstanding submarines during the early stages of the war.

I have always had a profound respect and unlimited admiration for our people who travel under the sea. They are a rough and hungry lot. They have played a major role in the war in the Pacific by severing the enemy's lifeline of shipping and destroying large units of Japan's Imperial Fleet.

The incidents related in these pages bring out the traditions and superstitions of submariners, their comradeship and sociability, the making over of a group of men from various and sundry sources into an integral unit, and the give-and-take life they lead.

The successes of the *Seawolf* bear testimony to the effectiveness of single-purposeness and teamwork. They bore in, were offensive-minded when targets were there, and they called on all their cunning and skill to evade when the Jap was hurt and mad.

This book will impress you with something all Navy people accept as everyday truth. It is the way the captain carries his ship, how his personality and influence make themselves felt on every man-jack in his outfit.

Freddie Warder and his crew can play on my team anytime, anywhere. The people of our country are indeed fortunate to have on their side killers like the *Seawolf* crowd who have done a magnificent job from the very beginning. Every American can feel intensely proud of our submarines.

JONAS H. INGRAM
Admiral, U. S. Navy
Commander in Chief
U. S. Atlantic Fleet

Prologue

THIS BOOK really began one sultry Sunday afternoon in August 1943, on a slow train between New York City and New London, Connecticut. We saw him first. He was big and brawny, his giant frame squeezed into a coach seat; he had the clear blue eyes, the hawk-like gaze of a Viking; and he was the most beribboned figure we had ever seen in a navy uniform. I think we spent all of five minutes in a vain attempt to read his personal history from those colorful decorations over his heart. He was a submarine man, and he'd been in combat—that much was clear from the silver submarine pin which led the collection of campaign ribbons. He had been decorated for gallantry—that was the coveted red, white, and blue ribbon of the Silver Star to the left. That orange and blue ribbon below meant action in the Asiatic-Pacific theater; here was the Good Conduct ribbon, the American theater; stars, numerals, one, two, three major battles—but it was too much of a job. On his left sleeve, near the shoulder, were the enclosed gold chevrons of a chief petty officer and the crossed bolts of lightning which indicated a radioman. Clear enough, so far: he was a chief radioman in the United States submarine service, and he had done things and been places.

We were particularly interested in a submarine man at that time. We were bound for the U.S. Submarine Base in New London to take a training cruise in a submarine. As Navy-accredited correspondents, we had been given a pleasant newspaper assignment—to write a story on submarine training and to describe how it feels to descend fifty or a hundred feet under the sea.

We engaged our submarine man in conversation. His name was Eckberg—Joseph Melvin Eckberg. Chief radioman. From what submarine? He rubbed his nose and gave us a slow grin.

Well, anyway, we said—and we identified ourselves—if we obtained clearance from the Navy, would he tell us a little about his ship—where they'd been and what they'd done? Chief Radioman Eckberg, J.M., hemmed and hawed and looked uncomfortable. He wasn't one to talk, but if it would be all right with Washington ... he'd been on one of the greatest sea-raiders of all time, and Lord knows she made submarine history ...

We followed through and learned in Washington that Eckberg's ship was none other than the U.S.S. *Seawolf.* The *Seawolf?* Why, her epic feats against the Japs had already made her almost legendary wherever Navy men gathered. Up to now the Navy had dared only hint at her exploits. She had been identified by name in less than half a dozen cautious news dispatches ... if her story could be told now, at last ... all of which explains how it happened that a week later we found ourselves in the cozy parlor of one of the snug little two-story houses the Navy has built for its personnel in Navy Heights, Groton, Connecticut, overlooking the spanking waters of the Thames River, with Eckberg thumbing through clippings of the *Seawolf,* Mrs. Eckberg busy with the dishes in the kitchen, and the littlest Eckberg—David, called Spike, three years old, a chubby, towheaded candidate for Annapolis, class of 1962—laying on the floor with a heavy paperweight made from the same iron-hard teakwood that went into the deck of the *Seawolf.*

Here was a picture of the *Wolf's* commissioning on Dec. 1, 1939, her crew stiffly at attention, the flag blowing from the mast, a gray sky overhead. Here was a snapshot of the crew, bearded and grinning, hanging their clothes up to dry on a rope strung from the conning tower to the bow of the *Wolf,* somewhere between fabled Bali and Borneo; here a photograph of Eckberg himself, thirty pounds thinner, a shadow of the man, as he looked when he returned from the *Wolf's* most dangerous mission. Here was a clipping about the *Seawolf:*

> *... the daring raider ... the U.S. submarine that terrified the Japs in their own waters.*

Here was a second:

> *The submarine U.S.S. Seawolf... recent Pacific cruise that will go down in United States naval history as one of the epic stories of submarine warfare.*

Here, finally, was a third:

> *Washington, D.C., April 13.—The Navy emblazoned the names of slight, unassuming Lt. Commander Frederick Burdett Warder and his submarine Seawolf today on its mounting roll of honor. It was the 1,450 ton Seawolf, sister ship of the ill-fated Squalus, the Navy disclosed, which sank a ...*

But Eckberg was shaking his head. "That doesn't tell the story," he said.
"Why?" we asked.
He slammed his fist down on the table.
"Because, damn it, it doesn't tell the whole story. It doesn't explain why the *Seawolf* is the best damn submarine in the United States Navy. Why, down in Lombok Straits one night ..."
"Look," we said, "let's start from the beginning."
"Okay," he said. "Right from the beginning."
And this is the story.

CHAPTER I

This is the *Seawolf*

LET'S TAKE the *Wolf* the first time I saw her. She wasn't any beauty then. They were just completing her at Portsmouth, New Hampshire. She was covered with black scaffolding, workmen were climbing over her sides, and I felt low. You see, they were building the *Wolf* at Flatiron Pier on the Piscataqua River; and in the drydock, less than three hundred yards away, they'd brought in the ill-fated *Squalus*. For ten bad minutes before I set eyes on the *Wolf*, I watched them take the dead from the *Squalus*. I saw them carrying off the bodies of men I knew, lifeless bodies hidden under gray tarpaulins, carrying them over the gangplank on stretchers; and at the same time I heard the pneumatic hammers working on the hull of the *Wolf*, just out of sight around the river's bend. I don't get shaky easy, but, standing there, you couldn't help think a little about life and death.

The *Squalus*, which hadn't come up from a test dive, a floating tomb for so many men; and the *Seawolf*, all fresh and new and ready to go out and make a name for herself, as the *Squalus* had hoped to do ...

When I finally got away from there and stood in front of the *Wolf*, I did my best to keep the *Squalus* out of my mind. Yard workmen were laying the *Wolf*'s teakwood decking, riveters were assembling her periscope shears, painters were daubing a thick black coat of paint on her sides, which swelled outward so gracefully at the waterline. Her heavy bronze bell was being rigged. Under the scaffolding I could make out her clean, trim lines. She was pretty.

Watching, thinking about it all, I couldn't know then what lay before us—Cavite and the stench of Jap dead in the harbor of Manila; the looting of the Philippines; terror and split-second escapes from death in the shallow waters of the Lombok Straits; day and night raids on Jap shipping from Christmas Island to Corregidor; depth charges and depth charges and depth charges—many missions and 40,000 miles under the Pacific, and weeks on end without seeing the sun—well, nobody could have dreamed of anything like that, then. It was August 1939, and the newspapers that day were full of the threat of war.

I'd come to Portsmouth that morning from San Diego, where I'd been advanced in rank to radioman, first class, and transferred from the U.S.S. *Plunger*. Months earlier, in Pearl Harbor, I'd put in for the *Seawolf* when I learned she was being built, and they had told me that if I was selected, I'd sail under Lieutenant Commander Frederick Warder, of Grafton, West Virginia. He'd been in charge of outfitting the *Wolf* from the beginning. I learned now that he was laid up with a bad knee. Less than an hour after I'd seen the *Wolf*, I knocked at his door on the second floor of the hospital in the Navy Yard.

A soft voice with just the trace of a drawl said, "Come in," and I walked in. He was in bed. I introduced myself. He looked up at me with the steadiest blue eyes I've ever seen. "Eckberg, eh?" he said. "Radioman?"

"Yes, sir," I said. "I got in today. They told me you had a bad knee. I've just been transferred from the *Plunger*."

"Good!" said Captain Warder heartily. "I'm glad to see you."

I was to learn that "Good!" was his favorite expression. Had we sunk a Jap man-of-war? Good! Were we winning or losing? Good! If the first, we'll do better still; if the second, we'll come back twice as hard.

He struggled to sit up. I helped him. He was a small, trim man, almost schoolteacher-ish in appearance, but with authority in every gesture. He appeared to be four or five years older than I was—say about thirty-five. Firm lips, determined chin, piercing blue eyes under narrowed lids, smooth face. I'd learned about him. Graduate of Annapolis, 1925; graduate, M.S. in engineering, University of California, 1934; submarine engineer; married, father of four children—a competent citizen of the United States Navy.

"This knee of mine," he began, and with an effort he swung about and sat on the edge of the bed. "It's been bothering me ever since I slipped on the ice last winter." He looked me up and down and suddenly began firing questions. "Have you seen the *Wolf* yet?"

"Just a little while ago, Captain," I said.

"How do you like her?"

I told him. I liked her lines. She looked clean.

"She's a damn fine boat!" he said, and that was that.

As for me, why had I been transferred? Had I asked for a new boat? Why? What sort of radio gear did I have on the *Plunger?* Was I familiar with this type and that? His questions were direct. As head radio and sound man on the *Wolf*, I'd be her eyes and ears under water. A submarine is blind below periscope depth, and her only contact with the world is by sound. She feels and gropes her way along the bottom of the sea, between shoals, over reefs—all by sound. She recognizes the enemy's approach by sound and measures the success of her attacks by sound.

I answered his questions.

"Good!" he said finally, and gave me my first order. "Go down to the *Seawolf* and look around. Dig for information. You'll have plenty of time. *Learn that boat.* Go there after the yard workmen knock off, and they won't bother you. But learn that boat."

"Aye, aye, Captain," I said. "I sure will."

"Very well, Eckberg," he said. He smiled. "I'll be seeing you."

In the Navy "Aye, aye" means "I have heard your order and will attend to it," and "Very well" means "I have heard what you have said and acknowledge it." We'd hit it off right, Captain Warder and I, at the very beginning.

That night, as we had supper in the dinette of the small furnished house we'd taken in Portsmouth, I told my wife, Marjorie, about it. Marjorie is blonde and slender and good-natured and blessed with common sense. She grew up in Chicago, met me when I was still a third-class radioman, and, in spite of the gloomy warnings of her friends and my own irresponsibility, married me. She liked music and she liked the sea. She was proud to be a Navy wife. In the five years of our marriage she had never complained of the haphazard life we'd led. But I knew the *Squalus* tragedy had hit her hard. She listened silently as I talked about the *Wolf,* and told her how impressed I was with the calm sureness and friendliness of my new skipper. She poured the coffee. "Is he married?" she asked.

I grinned. I knew Marjorie. Like all navy wives, she felt better if she knew her husband's skipper was married and had a family waiting at home for him. They like to think that tends to make a captain keep both feet on the ground and not take needless risks.

"Yes," I said. "Married and with four children, too."

Marjorie looked out the window. Through that window, on a clear day, you could see Portsmouth Harbor. You could see the Isle of Shoals; you could see the submarines as they went out to sea and took their first dives. It was off the Isle of Shoals that the *Squalus* dived.

"Well," she said, "I suppose that will give me more peace of mind. I don't think I'll ever forget the men on the *Squalus.* I want a husband that's alive, Mel."

The crew of the *Wolf* began to gather now—picked submarine men from all over the world, from San Diego and Mare Island, China and New London, Panama and Seattle—burly men, ham-fisted and barrel-chested; little wiry men who looked as though they'd jump at a noise but turned out to be made of cold-drawn steel; soft-looking men who could bake a cake or strangle a man; psalm-singers and book-lovers; swaggering lady-killers and men with ice-water in their veins; Jew and Gentile, Italian, Swede, Dane, German, Scotch, Irish, Pole—Americans who were to take over the *Wolf* with me and make her the great searaider she was, one of the greatest of all time. These are submarine men. They know how to keep their hands busy and their mouths shut. They're tough-muscled and tough-minded. They size each other up quickly. A hearty clasp of the hand, a swift appraisal, a grin. "I was on the *S-41.*" —"Hell, no! Jesus, you must know my old buddy, Duke Briggs."—"Know him? Why ..." Hand clasps, old stories revived, new friendships made.

Most of us meet in the Submarine Barracks, Building 150, assigned to the *Seawolf's* crew. Here, eight hours a day, we study blueprints of the *Wolf.* A submarine such as the *Wolf* needs a crew of 65—three complete crews each on an eight-hour shift, and specialists all. Officers, electricians, machinists, radiomen, firemen, signalmen, torpedomen, fire-controlmen, cooks, mess boys. The *Wolf* has to be our home, a battleship on the surface, a raider under the surface, able to hold her own against anything on the sea, below it or above it.

The men come in, their white canvas seabags over their shoulders, their grips in their hands. They ask, "Is this where the *Seawolf* bunks?"

We glance up from our blueprints. "This is it," we say. We look them over carefully. They throw their bags down.

"Well, this is the place, then," one says. "Any empty bunks? How about a locker?"

We're the crew of the *Seawolf*. We learn who our officers will be. Executive and Navigation Officer, second in command, is Lieutenant William Nolin Deragon of Albany, New York, Annapolis '34, a tall, rangy man with a long face etched with two sharp lines from nose to mouth, and deep-set eyes. He's just come off the *S-42*. He's completely nerveless, calm in the most dangerous situation. He will become "Willie" to Captain Warder. The phrase, "Now, Willie, what I want"—the Skipper's usual preface to an order, whether it be to attack a Jap destroyer or to find a case of iced beer for the crew in some desolate tropical outpost—is to become a familiar one to us all.

Diving officer is Ensign, later Lieutenant, Richard Holden, of Rutland, Vermont, Annapolis '37, handsome, black-haired, energetic, with a deep bass voice. He's only twenty-four, but he already has the respect of his men. Communications Officer is Ensign James Mercer of White Plains, New York, a University of Michigan man, slim, aquiline-nosed, with thick black brows, retiring— everything a Navy officer should be. He's a model to the crew, absolutely fearless. As Communications Officer he's the Skipper's right hand during an attack.

Day by day the rest of the crew gathers. Chief Torpedoman Robert ("Squeaky") Langford, a thirty-five-year-old lanky Iowan with a high-pitched voice and a complete knowledge of a torpedo's temperament; Ensign Burr Casler, Assistant Navigation Officer, whose jutting jaw and wiry thatch of hair make him look twice as pugnacious as he is; Chief Pharmacist's Mate Frank Loaiza, "doctor" of the *Wolf*, a dark, handsome, nervous Puerto Rican who talks with his hands and will be forever hurrying through the boat to his cabinet in the after-battery, getting medicine for us—saline tablets, aspirins, laxatives. He's "Pill-roller" and the "Quack" to us, but he takes our kidding good-naturedly.

I meet Chief Yeoman John Edward Sullivan, thirty-two, from New Jersey, a big, blond, ruddy-faced Irishman who is to be the *Wolf*'s chief clerk, keeping the files, the war diary, and all necessary data. Edward ("Pop") Mocarsky— forty-three, with a few wisps of gray hair on top of his head, a sober, silent Pole from East Hartford, Connecticut, an old-school electrician whose "Mocarsky circuits" baffle any other electrician. Chief Torpedoman Edward Sousa, chief petty officer of the boat, who could rouse the dead with his booming voice; and

Electrician's Mate Hank Brengelman, a roly-poly German with pale blue eyes and a love for books; and Chief Machinist's Mate Otis C. Dishman, at thirty-eight a legendary figure in the submarine service, a powerfully built man who looks vaguely like Orson Welles made up for a terrifying part, and whose tattoo designs—flowers, pretty girls, and rushing railroad trains speeding about his body—are equally famous among sub men.

These are the men of the *Seawolf*. We consider ourselves a damn fine crew. We know we're different from other services of the armed forces. We differ from the crew of a Flying Fortress, for example, or a company of Marines, because we have no identity outside our submarines. We were not salesmen, clerks, factory employees, white-collar workers, transformed overnight into fighting men. Most of us have had no private life. Most of us went into the Navy as soon as we were old enough—seventeen, eighteen, nineteen. With all due modesty we know we're picked men, paid 50 percent more in our jobs than men in any other branch of the service, and that few of us will be in it actively after we're forty—because it's so tough. Most of us have been in submarine service for at least ten years. Most of us are married, with families. Submarines are our lives and our careers. We've never been interviewed by newspaper writers. We've never talked about what we've done.

We'd never thought there was much to talk about. But, then, we hadn't been on the *Seawolf*. We hadn't become part of a boat that was glory itself.

My first trip through the *Wolf* was unforgettable. I thought I knew submarines. I'd been on the boats for twelve years, since I was eighteen, when my brother Paul, quartermaster first class on a submarine, felt my biceps, punched me in the shoulder, and said, "Kid, why don't you come into this outfit? We could use you."

In twelve years I'd seen a lot of submarines, but the *Wolf* topped them all. More than 308 feet long, weighing 1,480 tons, built to make over 20 knots surface speed, air-conditioned and equipped with every modern device, she combined the best we knew in submarine construction.

I ducked into her conning tower and let myself down the narrow perpendicular steel ladder leading to the control room directly under it. I turned around—and whistled. I'd never seen so many instruments—dials, valves, gauges, controls—in one control room. The room was white, glistening white, and the instruments shone and gleamed. I almost swelled with pride as I stood there and drank it all in. Here was the glittering "Christmas Tree," a small panel of green and red lights which gave the legend on every hatch of the *Wolf*, and whether it was open or closed. Here was the depth gauge, here the two tremendous wheels which operated the bow and stern planes, the fin-like projections on either side of the *Wolf* controlling her balance underwater; the high-pressure manifolds, which drive thousands of gallons of water out of her tanks to send her to the surface, or suck in a small flood to weight her down and send her deep; the helmsman's wheel—all the magic-working buttons, wheels and levers of a modern submarine. In one corner was a head, or toilet, in its tiny compartment, one of the four on the ship; and in the opposite corner of the control room, set off in a compartment by itself, was the radio and sound room—my shack.

Here was my station. It was about six by eight feet, just enough room for three men, and dominated by my radio gear—sets of intricate apparatus that looked like the control board of a radio station, with a panel six feet high and four feet wide rising from the back of a glass-topped table. Behind me, as huge and fully as intricate, my sound gear. Above, and to the left, a shelf for reference books. Overhead, the wires and rows of cables and tubing that mark almost every inch of ceiling space in a submarine.

Seated at this table—my desk—I had before and behind me the last word in submarine radio and sound gear, an instrument of electrical echo-ranging and sonic devices so sensitive that when the *Wolf* was submerged I would be able to detect the beating of a ship's screws when she was still far away. On the surface I'd switch from sound to radio, and send and receive with antenna strung topside.

I explored further. I squeezed through the oval bulkhead doorway—if you were over six feet tall you had to bend almost double to go through—and found myself in the narrow passageway leading to the forward torpedo room, in the bow. It was hardly wide enough for two men to squeeze by each other. As I went forward, here on the left was the chief petty officer's stateroom; then the captain's stateroom, with desk, depth gauge fitted into the wall, gyrocompass repeater, night-bell to call his messboys.

Next, the officers' wardroom, where they ate, held conferences, played cards, lounged—scarcely as large as the dinette of a small apartment; and then a tiny pantry with a serving shelf opening into the wardroom. There'd always be a messboy here to turn out sandwiches and coffee for the officers, day and night.

On the opposite side of the passageway was the yeoman's or ship's office, with typewriter, stainless steel file, and cabinets; this would be Sully's domain. Then came the engineering officer's stateroom, to be shared by Holden and Mercer. Like a pullman compartment, it had two settees which could be turned into bunks at night. Then the executive officer's stateroom—and then another head and a shower room. After this, the forward torpedo room. Directly ahead of me were the round brass doors of the four bow torpedo tubes. This forward torpedo room was a large room, at least fifty feet long by fifteen feet wide. Suspended on heavy chains from the ceiling, at least seven feet from the floor, were six bunks, three on either side. Under them were the torpedo racks, now empty, but later to be filled with the burnished bronze-steel torpedoes, two tons each, lying side by side in tiers.

In the center of the room four "jump" bunks—so called because men could jump out of them, dismantle them, and pull them out of the way in a minute or less. I looked this room over carefully.

14

A face bowl and a towel rack came out of the wall. Here were blowers, ventilators leading from our air-conditioning plant. Large, too. If the size of the blower pipes meant anything, there'd be a lot of air in this room. Well, I thought, I'll try to get me a bunk here.

I retraced my steps. I ducked back down the passageway, through the control room again, and found myself in the afterpart of the *Wolf*. First, the after-battery compartment. Here most of the crew would live. The metal clothing lockers were already installed. I pushed on, through a doorway, and was in the mess hall.

Three tables were set, across the width of the boat, each with a rim to keep dishes from sliding off when the *Wolf* pitched. A bulletin board was already in place on one wall. I opened a door on my left. This was a small provisions room. I passed the refrigerator.

The next doorway I found on one side turned out to be the door to the galley. Four-coil electric stove, with two ovens; a huge coffee urn; a sink; a Mixmaster for pastries; pots and pans neatly packed into shelves; bins for coffee, flour, sugar—the whole thing no larger than a kitchenette, compact and efficient enough! I'd never know how sixty-five men could be served three meals a day, sandwiches and snacks and hot coffee and hot soup day and night—all from this little room.

Next to the galley was the scullery, where the mess cooks would grumble about their low station while doing dishes by the carload. Opposite the scullery, a wash and shower room—two showers, four face bowls, mirrors, lockers for soap and toothpaste. So far, so good. I ducked back further. Now I was in the forward engine room, then the aft engine room, both with their powerful Diesels, like some endless-cylindered motor of some thirtieth-century racing machine; then the after-torpedo room in the stern, a replica of the forward torpedo room. Toilet on the port side of the after engine room, shower on the starboard side. Compactness, utility, efficiency—that was the *Seawolf*.

For weeks we grew with the *Wolf*. Captain Warder, his knee better, joined us in Building 150 as we pored over blueprints. With the crew and workmen he crawled all over the *Wolf* as well. We were proud of our skipper; not every submarine crew could boast that their captain was also a submarine engineer who knew his boat from the keel up. Sometimes, at the end of the day, he came into Building 150 looking like a grease-pit mechanic, but there'd be the light of discovery in his eyes. He'd ask for a cup of coffee. There'd be a silence. He'd stir his coffee slowly. "Well," he'd say, "I found out something new today."

"What was that, Captain?" someone would ask.

"You know that fuel line running along the port side of the forward engine room?" he'd say. "It has a flange right at Number 105 bulkhead. I didn't know that." He'd sip his coffee thoughtfully. "That might come in useful someday."

We thrashed over every pipe and line, every induction coil and bulkhead. Afternoons we spent studying the *Wolf* herself. We went into the ship, and we underwent "dry dives." The lights would suddenly go out, leaving us in complete blackness; the command would ring out for each of us to take a new station. I might find myself at the Christmas Tree, in the radio shack, at a torpedo tube—anywhere. Each of us had to know as much as possible about every other man's job. Every submarine man is a specialist, but he must be prepared to take over any other post at a moment's notice, whether it be frying eggs or firing torpedoes.

We learned to take apart and put together practically everything but the hull of the *Wolf*. We had to draw thirty-four blueprints of her principal systems. By the time we completed our schoolwork we knew the anatomy of the *Wolf* as a surgeon knows the muscles and their insertions, the bones and their functions, the arteries and their positions.

We began to move into the submarine. The first thing I did was to paste a photograph of Marjorie on the panel of my sound gear, and fix another above my bunk, which turned out to be No.1 bunk, in the forward torpedo room—just where I wanted it. My locker was built into the bulkhead next to my bunk, and I packed away my clothing: four suits of blue dungarees; four changes of underwear, one set of gray wool, one heavy all-wool with double back and chest; a dozen pair of socks, six wool, six cotton; two pairs of black shoes; dress and undress blues; sandals; six hats (blue and white, and one warm blue knitted watch cap for cold nights on deck).

Throughout the ship my shipmates began to move in, too. Squeaky Langford came aboard with a miniature Chinese carved teakwood chest he'd picked up in Sing Tow. It was a good-luck charm, and in it he had his good conduct medal, a couple of old rings minus stones, and a broken watch. Men came aboard with their St. Christopher's medals and crucifixes. There was a Bible or two. They came with their pipes and tobacco, their favorite magazines, batches of letters they wanted to show off, photographs, acey-deucy sets, dice, decks of cards. We married men pasted up snapshots of our families inside our locker doors. Neat green curtains were hung in the doorways of the officers' staterooms. Life jackets and Momsen lungs were stowed into place in the bulkheads. Dishman showed up with a portable phonograph which he gave a place of honor on a workbench in the engine room. Books—Jack London's sea stories, biographies, Zane Grey's stories—began to fill the double bookshelf in the mess hall, which for no reason at all suddenly became "Kelly's Pool Room." Henry ("Short Pants") Hershey—"Short Pants" because he was five feet four—a machinist's mate and a wizard softball player, came in lugging a sackful of bats, balls, and mitts. We were making the *Wolf* our home.

On a cold February 15, with a chill wind blowing the waters of the bay white and black, Marjorie drove me into the yard and down to the dock. The *Wolf* was to go out on her first sea dive. Marjorie was to drive me down, then return. From our window she would look out on the entrance channel and lower harbor, and watch the *Wolf* go out, and go down. We rounded a turn, and the submarine came into sight. Black, shining black, in the cold morning sun, long, sleek, and black—a magnificent engine of destruction. She rode heavy in the water alongside the slate-colored drydock. There was tremendous activity topside, and a crowd of navy yard workmen and navy wives waiting to see us off. The deck force was scampering about, chopping the ice clear from our lines, and even in the distance the orders echoed crisp and clear. I made out Lieutenant Holden at once. He was standing well up on the bow, the wind whipping his heavy submarine coat. The flag was blowing at the stern. I got out of the car.

"Well, here goes, honey," I said.

"Oh, Mel," she said. I leaned down and kissed her. She turned the wheel sharply and drove off. I came aboard the *Wolf* as a voice boomed through a megaphone from the bridge: "Preparations for getting under way!"

There was a terrific roar from deep within the *Wolf*; then a series of sharp, ear-splitting reports, like a 20-mm. gun firing. Her powerful Diesels were turning over.

From the bridge, the same booming voice: "Stations for getting under way!"

The gangway was hauled in; the crew sprang to action.

"Take in No. 4!" came from the bridge. "Take in No. 4!" another voice echoed. The heavy two-inch lines were hauled in swiftly. They were brittle with ice, and they snapped and bit at the air as they were pulled and fed hand over hand through a hatch into the after-torpedo room.

"Take in No. 3!" came the order, and "Take in No. 3!" came the echo.

The crew worked as one man; the Captain took his place on the bridge. As Line No. 1 was loosened and pulled in, the stationary colors were brought down, the running colors climbed up the mast. The *Wolf* was free of everything that held her to the land.

Her engines purred. Thick black smoke poured from the exhausts along the waterline.

The familiar odor of burned fuel oil came to me, and the old excitement swept over me. I hurried into the radio shack; I put on my earphones; the intercommunication system was switched on, and all through the *Wolf*'s compartments little grilled loud-speakers awoke and chattered. When the Captain went into the conning tower, not a whisper of his but echoed through the ship. We were all one family, all wrapped together in that extraordinary intimacy of men who go down to the sea in the sealed steel chambers of a submarine.

The good-byes rang out in the crisp air. The *Wolf*'s engines raced into a deafening roar. Slowly, stern first, streams of white water pouring from her sides and into the darker waters of the bay, she slid away from the dock and into the channel.

Engines thundering now, we cleared the outer harbor. We neared the Isle of Shoals, where the *Squalus* met her doom.

"Rig for dive." Captain Warder's order was almost casual.

"Rig for dive" ran tinnily through the boat. From stern to bow men leaped to their stations, spinning wheels, pulling controls, bracing themselves against valves. For a full ten minutes men investigated, inspected, tested, readying the *Wolf* for her dive.

Lieutenant Holden's deep bass voice echoed through the intercommunications. "Main induction has been tested, bow and stern planes tested, safety flooded, sir."

"Very well," came Captain Warder's voice. "Stand by to dive."

"Stand by to dive," echoed back.

Two sharp blasts of the diving alarm. Slowly, like some prehistoric aquatic monster, the *Seawolf* buried her nose in the water, and, moving ever forward, nudged her way deeper, deeper, until the waters closed over her and she vanished from sight.

We wasted no time putting the *Wolf* through her paces. Drill followed drill, dive followed dive. We had to anticipate every emergency. We assumed the *Wolf* was in a collision; that she had caught on fire; that she was being shelled; that her hull had been stove in; that she was being depth-charged. In a practice dive off the Isle of Shoals, the drill order came: "Power gone on the bow and stern planes. Shift to hand." We were assuming that our electrical power had suddenly gone, and that the boat had to be taken down by manual power alone. The bow- and stern-planes men instantly shifted to hand operation, maneuvering the planes by means of the huge wheels, each as wide as two men abreast. But within thirty seconds Dishman, on the bowplanes, shouted, "I can't hold her!" Strongest man on the boat, his tremendous back muscles stood out and perspiration poured down his sides as he struggled with the wheel. The *Wolf* was knifing her way downward so swiftly that the water pressure made it impossible for him to shift the planes back. Two men leaped to his assistance. They couldn't budge it. We were taking a terrific angle on the bow; the bowplanes were jammed at "hard dive," and my chair began sliding forward. I clung to my desk. Captain Warder rushed down the control-room ladder.

"Blow No. 1!" he ordered. The high-pressure air screamed into the tank, emptying it of water. Our eyes were glued to the depth gauge—90 ... 100 ... 150 ... 170 feet ... We braced ourselves. We had only 230 feet of water here. The *Squalus* flashed through my mind. If we were to strike a rock ledge on the bottom ...

Captain Warder, his eyes darting from the gauge to the men straining frantically at the wheel and back again, snapped: *"Blow everything!"*

We were emptying every tank we had!

Still the *Wolf* went down. 180 feet ... 200 feet ...

"All back, emergency!"

It was the order to reverse propellers—the last resort of a submarine captain. "All back, emergency!" echoed over the phones from the maneuvering space.

The *Seawolf* shuddered. Slowly she checked her descent. Slowly, as her propellers bit into the water and pulled the stern down, she came to an even keel. My chair began sliding back. But now the *Wolf* began to rise, faster and faster, until with terrific speed she popped out on the surface of the sea like a cork in a dishpan. Our eardrums clicked. Fog set in through the ship as the water in the air expanded in the lowered pressure. We peered hazily at each other.

"Open the hatch!"

The fresh air rushed in.

Someone said, "Christ, I was wondering if I was ever going to smell that filthy stuff again!"

We breathed deeply. We had been down far, and now we were up; and the *Wolf* was still as good as new.

The *Wolf's* shakedown cruise—to shake down or shake out the bugs in her system—began April 12, 1940. From Portsmouth to Galveston, to Tampa, to Corpus Christi, to Cristobal, Canal Zone, to the Brooklyn Navy Yard, to Annapolis, and back to Portsmouth again—a two-months trip to test her under every possible condition.

At the same time the crew was put to the test. We grew to know each other better, to learn each other's habits of work.

Teamwork is the essence of a submarine, and only by endless and incessant practice through one maneuver to another can a crew acquire perfection, so that they can tumble out of their bunks and click into split-second precision almost the instant an alarm sounds. Each of us became letter-perfect in our stations. Before, in our training periods, we had learned to know the *Wolf*—every cubbyhole, every cable. Now we learned to mesh together.

Our stations, our duties, were as clear-cut as the assignments given a crack football team in a championship game. Life was the title we were fighting for, and death always lurked as the penalty for a man who wasn't where he should be, for a man offside. We couldn't afford to make mistakes, and officers and men moved, transferred, replaced each other, with clockwork regularity.

Lieutenant Holden, engineering officer, dove the boat and was in charge of all machinery. Ensign Mercer, communications officer, decoded messages, handled confidential publications, was ordered to guard with his life the *Wolf's* secret U.S. Navy codebook.

Sousa, chief petty officer, was liaison man between officers and enlisted men. We learned that Ensign Casler was a poor cribbage player, but an expert navigation officer; that Dishman rarely failed in an emergency; that Sully had a knack for baking cakes; that Loaiza was always complaining that he was afraid and always proving the opposite. We grew to know Captain Warder, to learn how precise and accurate a technician he was, and how human.

One afternoon some of us were on the Cigarette Deck, the afterpart of the bridge, listening to a portable radio. We were sitting on wooden benches and lounging about, absorbing the sun.

Captain Warder climbed up from below. He was wearing shorts and undershirt and sandals.

"Hello, boys," he said affably. And without further ado he began setting up exercises to the music. He stood there in the sun, unconcerned, arms up, arms down, bend, rise, one, two, three; one, two, three, in time to the music, giving himself the commands a little more breathlessly each time, until he was out of breath. We couldn't help chuckling.

"Go ahead and laugh," he said. "You'll never see me with a bay window."

After that, he went up on deck each afternoon when he could, and exercised. He knew how cruelly confinement can work on your body, making your legs weak, your feet swollen, your back aching, until a mile's walk on land becomes torture.

Back in Portsmouth the *Wolf* received her post-shakedown overhauling. Errors in construction, defects in gears, leakages, were corrected. She was trimmed, tightened, tuned. In September we left for Newport, Rhode Island. There, for six weeks, day after day, we had extensive torpedo practice. The torpedo crews sent practice fish crashing into fictional destroyers. Nothing was overlooked. Then to New London, Connecticut, where we spent hours practicing escapes with Momsen lungs. The *Wolf* had proved herself; we had to prove ourselves. In peacetime, submarine crews are like boxers between bouts. They are forever in training. The fight may never come, but they train as if it were to come any moment. There are competitions and contests to keep them on their toes. Each submarine competes for records in engineering, gunnery, torpedo marksmanship, communications—every phase of submarine activity.

Marjorie had been expecting our first baby; and in April, shortly after I left with the *Wolf* on her shakedown cruise, Marjorie went to San Diego to rent a house, furnish it as our permanent home, and await the baby's arrival. In New London I waited expectantly for word from San Diego. It came in October. I had no inkling of what it was when I took it, myself, in the radio shack. In Morse code a message came in. It was the Submarine Base, New London, calling the *Seawolf*. I answered, "Go ahead." Again the formal letters. And then, as I took down the words on my typewriter, the message spelled itself out:

> *"Launching-took-place-this-morning-early.*
> *It's-a-stem-winder.*
> *Fully-equipped.*
> *Marge-had-an-easy-time. She-misses-you-dreadfully.*
> *Congrats. Dutch."*

I ripped the sheet out of my typewriter and bellowed, "It's a boy! It's a boy!"

Heads popped. Somebody started hammering on a bulkhead.

"Where are the cigars?" a voice growled.

The hand of war reached out to touch us first on Friday, November 15, 1940. We were in San Diego, Marjorie, Spike—our five-weeks-old youngster, christened David—and the *Seawolf*.

The *Wolf* had come in on Wednesday from New London. We had all been granted a five-day leave, and for the first time in months Marjorie and I were enjoying a normal family life, now made more wonderful by Spike's presence. About 10 a.m. on Friday the doorbell rang. It was Sully. He had his hat in his hand, and he looked uncomfortable.

"Eck," he said, "you got to get back to the boat."

"What!" I demanded. "We just got here!"

"I know," he said. "But those are the orders. I've got instructions to round up everybody."

I led the way into the living room. Marjorie was bathing Spike in the kitchen, and I could hear them cooing and laughing together. I left Sully sitting on the edge of the sofa, and I went into the kitchen, trying to think what to say. When I saw Marjorie and Spike together, so happy, I didn't have the heart to tell her.

I said, "It's Sully. It's pay day, and I told them to let it ride; but I guess they want me back to pay me."

She looked up, and I think she knew I wasn't telling the truth.

She knew Sully wouldn't have come all the way out to see me for that.

"All right," she said. "Get back as soon as you can."

Sully came into the kitchen, and, fast-thinking Irishman that he was, he knew what to do and say. He strode over to the bathenet and put his arm around Marjorie, and then tickled Spike under the chin.

"What are you trying to do?" he demanded, turning to me.

"You're always telling me he has red hair. Why, it's almost white."

I left them talking together and went upstairs to put on my blues. I didn't take my seabag along, so that I'd have reason to return and say good-by.

A few minutes after Sully and I reached the *Wolf* we were called to quarters. Lieutenant Deragon stepped up. He was a family man himself, with one child, and he knew what effect the news he was about to tell would have on us. He cleared his throat and said, "We're leaving tomorrow. Destination unknown. I can't tell you the hour. Now go ashore, conclude your business, and be aboard at 6:30 a.m."

Marjorie and I did little that last night but sit around and ogle Spike. We couldn't get our fill of him. We put him on the carpet, and he lay on his back gurgling. We watched him until he fell asleep out of sheer weariness. Then we put him to bed and began to pack. It was just as well that we kept him up so late. The next time I saw my son he was two and a half years old.

While we packed I began to feel homesick—the first time in my life that I was homesick *before* going off. The last thing I placed in my bag was Spike's photograph. That would have a place of honor next to Marjorie's on my radio gear.

We were up at 5 a.m. the next morning. It was raining. Marjorie insisted upon walking down to the streetcar stop with me.

Then I had a feeling, a powerful hunch that it would be a long, long time before I'd see her again. I had a sinking feeling that I would never see her again. I fought to shake it out of my mind.

"Keep your chin up," I said. "I'll write every chance I get. Watch out for Spike. Don't let him know you're worried."

She managed a smile. "I'm not worried," she said, lying to my face. "I'm not worried a bit. You can take care of yourself."

I told her, "Why, you'll probably be riding a transport out to Pearl in a few weeks, and I'll see you there before you know it."

For some reason, we assumed we were going to Pearl Harbor.

And, waiting there in the rain, we both lied to each other. We talked about what I would do as soon as I got to Pearl. I'd look for a nice house. Five rooms would do. We talked about how much rent we could afford to pay—we settled on $35 a month, furnished.

The streetcar came. I said, "Well, I'll be seeing you, honey."

Her last words were, "I've got my fingers crossed, darling."

Then she began to cry. "Now, now," I said, awkwardly, and got into the car. I had a small handbag. The streetcar was empty except for one old man, probably a night watchman on his dreary way home, and I sat in the rumbling car, saying to myself, "I wonder when I'll be riding a San Diego streetcar again. I think I'm headed for places I've never seen before."

We shoved off that Saturday morning, November 16. Five days later we arrived at Pearl Harbor. There was nothing there then, a year before the Japanese attack, to indicate that this bustling U.S. naval base, more than 2,000 miles from San Francisco, would be marked for the first blow in the greatest war in history.

We were there only briefly, and we picked up two new members of the crew. I was in the control room when a thin, hollow-cheeked, dark-faced fellow, with dark eyes and a sardonic grin on his lips, climbed down. He was wearing dungarees and smoking one of the largest and smelliest corncob pipes I'd ever seen or suffered with.

"You on here?" I asked.

He nodded. "Just came aboard," he said. He looked around critically. "Damn nice boat," he said.

"You know, we're only here for a little while," I said. "We're due out fast."

He grinned a crooked grin I was to know and like after a while.

"I think I know where we're going," he said, "and that's where I want to go. I'm too close to the States now. My name's Zirkle."

I introduced myself. "Well, where are we headed?"

"West, buddy, west—Asiatic stations," he said mysteriously, and ducked aft to the mess room. That was my first introduction to the official pessimist of the *Wolf* and the loneliest man aboard. Zirk never talked about it, but the story was that he had a Chinese wife and children trapped somewhere in occupied China.

Later in the day, as I was bent over my radio reports, a dapper young fellow stuck his head in. "Eckberg here?" he asked.

"That's me," I said.

He stuck out his hand. "I'm your new radioman," he said. "My name's Paul Maley."

He was replacing a man who had been advanced in rank and transferred to another ship. He was small and dark, with a determined chin, a wide mouth, a long thin nose, and, for a man, the prettiest eyes I'd ever seen.

"O.K.," I said. "Do you know anything about this gear?"

He looked it over. "I'm not so hot," he admitted. He was about twenty-three, and I liked him at once. "But I can learn," he added.

"It certainly is a clean and snug-looking shack you have here."

I thought it was, too. It had been painted and decorated since the first time I'd walked through the *Wolf*. The antenna systems, the direction-finder apparatus, the entire interior, ceiling and bulkheads, were painted white. But there was color, too. Beside my chair we had a small stool, part wastepaper basket, about a foot high, with a bright green leather cushion. I had a black typewriter resting in the well of my glass-covered desk. To set off the desk, I'd put some bright blue blotting paper under the glass.

Green linoleum had been laid on the deck. All in all, with Marjorie's and Spike's photographs high on the panel, and the radio and technical books on the bookshelf, it was a cozy little room.

"This is a good ship," I said. "She's not thoroughly clean yet, but that's not the crew's fault. We're all working to make her pretty and pretty she'll be. She's going to be a real showboat. Come on, I'll show you where your bunk is." I took him into the forward torpedo room and showed him his bunk facing mine.

"O.K., Eck," he said, and that was the way it has always been between us— calm, easy, friendly, like two brothers. Maley and I worked side by side. During attacks it would be Paul's duty to keep a lookout for enemy ships while I concentrated on the target.

The crew of the *Wolf* had a special job in Pearl Harbor. We washed our clothes when we found the time and pressed our dress uniforms—whites and blues—on the mess hall tables with a small electric iron which we'd all chipped in to buy. The problem of what to do with soiled clothes, with long trips ahead of us, had to be solved. Sully had an inspiration.

"What we need is a washing machine, an electric one like I've got home."

We appointed a committee which called on the skipper. He said, "That's a damn fine idea. Go ahead."

We had a bank aboard the *Wolf*, called the *Seawolf*'s Slush Fund. If you were short of money and were going on liberty, you borrowed from the bank against your next pay day. You repaid with interest. Ten dollars cost you eleven dollars. Miss one payment, and you were taxed an additional dollar. This, with accumulated interest, was more than enough to pay for the washing machine.

Sully, as the moving spirit, and Mr. Deragon, representing the officers, went out to buy it. They walked into the biggest department store and, once inside, got into an argument as to which was married longer. The oldest husband in point of service should have the privilege of selecting the machine. As usual, Sully, who'd married at twenty-two, won the argument. He picked the machine—a gleaming white enameled beauty, big and round and perfect. It was delivered by ship's boat. Getting it down the hatch was a work of art. The entire ship's crew acted as sidewalk superintendents. When we finally squeezed it in, we didn't know where to place it. A submarine is built for efficiency, and there isn't any waste space. It could go into the washroom, but then there wouldn't be any room for anyone to get in and wash.

Sully said, "The hell with that. We'll change the washroom."

With that he set to work tearing down the hand-and-face bowls in the washroom in the mess hall, as well as mirrors, soap dishes, and towel racks. The auxiliary gang worked on this special assignment of love for three days, moving them all to the forward bulkhead of the washroom. Everyone, including the officers, took a hand helping them. One shower room was not much use anyway, since it was loaded up with soap powder and salt-water soap for Gus Wright and the mess cooks, and nobody used it because it was too much trouble to move out the stuff and then put it back again. We placed the washing machine in front of the shower, and there it stayed.

We christened it Baby, and she was one of the real heroes of the *Wolf*—actually, the only heroine aboard. She took all kinds of punishment without grumbling. She was coddled, she was cussed, she was depth charged, she was damned—and she was loved. She was not always innocent. Sometimes she developed a temper, sometimes she was impatient, and sometimes she was as unpredictable as a woman. There was the afternoon I spent a good part of an hour sewing three buttons on a pair of shorts. Baby made short shrift of my work—probably sheer feminine jealousy. When I took them out, they were minus the buttons. I must have stood there and cussed her for five minutes. But from then on Baby was our sewing critic. If she didn't rip off the buttons, you'd done a good job.

Before long the fore and aft part of the ship—the mechanics, or "Winton Wizards," and the deck force, or "Deck Apes," who were always competing against each other in baseball and liberty parties, were feuding about who could use Baby, and when, and why a clean machine like her had to take grease-stained dungarees in the first place.

Our second day at Pearl Harbor, Maley and I returned from town to find electricians spiking the *Wolf*'s batteries. I'd heard of this, but I'd never seen it before. It's an emergency measure to increase the speed and power of the boat, but at the expense of the battery's length of life. Since a submarine moves on battery power when it's submerged, only an emergency would compel the skipper to shorten the life of his batteries.

"This doesn't look so good," I said to Paul. "We're heading for trouble, sure."

The third day we took torpedoes aboard—not exercise torpedoes, but warheads. They went into place under my bunk.

There could be only one reason why we were getting war shots ready. That was to sink somebody. On the fifth night we pulled away from Pearl Harbor.

Now, for all practical purposes, we were on war service. The official declaration of war was still a year away, but our High Command was on the alert. We traveled with darkened ship; night lookouts were posted, four at a time, each to sweep one-fourth of the sea with powerful night glasses. We trained constantly; we were ready. The blow would come soon, no one knew when—but the *Seawolf* was ready.

CHAPTER II

The *Wolf* Strikes Back

MONDAY MORNING, December 8, 1941, the *Seawolf* lay in Manila Bay, anchored 600 yards from Cavite. We had been there for two weeks, waiting our turn to be overhauled. The port was as busy as a beehive with submarines. Two of them, the *Sea Lion* and *Sea Dragon*, our sister ships, were undergoing a complete yard overhaul. That meant removing all engines, tearing down the electrical systems, and then rebuilding the ship—a six- to eight-weeks job. The *Dragon* was almost completed, but the *Lion*'s engines were still lying on the dock. The *Wolf* was scheduled to go in for repairs on Thursday. We had quite a gathering there that day. Most of our Asiatic fleet, under Admiral Thomas C. Hart, was based in Manila Bay, its home port, and I should judge that at least thirty submarines were almost within shouting distance. Three submarine tenders—the *Holland,* the *Otus* and the *Canopus*—were on hand, too. They carried torpedoes, submarine spare parts, provisions, and stores. Admiral Hart himself was in Manila that day.

Jim Riley, an old shipmate of mine, and I were celebrating our reunion that weekend, and Monday morning found us in the outskirts of Manila with big heads. We needed a lot of black coffee. We climbed into a cab and made for the Plaza Café.

Around the corner of the restaurant we could pick up a bus for Cavite, twelve miles away.

We sat down at the counter. The Filipino boy looked as though he was going to bawl. "Hell, boy, what's the matter with you?" Jim demanded. He looked around. "What in hell is the matter with everybody? They're jumping around like a bunch of jitterbugs."

He was right. The place seemed to be seething with excitement.

The boy looked at us, startled. "You no hear Japs bomb Pearl Harbor?"

Pearl Harbor? U.S. soil? Jim and I stared at each other.

"You crazy?" I asked, turning to the Filipino. We glanced out the Plaza's big plate-glass window. People were hurrying by.

And suddenly we felt the tension, too. We dashed outside. A cab screeched to a stop. The driver poked his head out. "Going to the docks, sailor?" he asked.

"You hear anything about a bombing?" I demanded.

"Sure," said the driver. "You boys better wake up. I've been carrying Marines back to Cavite all morning."

"Well, hell!" I said. "Let's get going!" We piled into the cab. When we got to the dock everyone was rushing about. My heart leaped when I saw the *Wolf.* I caught a ship's boat out to her. On the way I saw the aircraft tender *Langley*, her helmeted gun crews manning anti-aircraft guns on her flight deck. Most of the *Wolf*'s crew was below when I finally got there. We were all a little punch drunk by the suddenness of it. Captain Warder, looking preoccupied, was already there. I was due topside for my watch, and I was pulling on my dungarees when Sousa walked through, his chin jutting out about an inch from where it should be.

"Come on, you guys, there's a war on," he growled. "Get moving!"

I climbed up the ladder fast. The air was mild, the sun shone.

War seemed impossible. Suddenly, in toward Manila, a light began blinking. It was our tender ship, the *Canopus*, signaling with her searchlight. She was about three miles away. I read the flashes, and with each word my blood pressure shot up.

> *"From ... Commander Asiatic Fleet ... To Asiatic Fleet...*
> *080820 ... Urgent... Break ... Japan ... has ... commenced*
> *... hostilities ... Govern ... yourselves ... accordingly."*

There it was, officially. From Admiral Hart himself.

Frank Franz, one of the signalmen, was on the bridge answering the *Canopus*, but I wanted to give the message to the Skipper immediately. I ran to the conning tower and shouted down, "Below!"

"What do you want?" boomed back.

"Tell the Captain urgent message came in from the Admiral. Japan has commenced hostilities."

The *Canopus*'s searchlight was blinking again. All sub captains were to come aboard at once for a conference. The Skipper hurried off. Lieutenant Deragon's high-pitched voice ran through the boat: "Preparations for getting under way."

I kept the watch on deck. I thought: *Those yellow sons of bitches. They're going to rate everything I can give them. Why haven't they shown up here? Those sons of bitches, those sons of bitches ...* and then a surge of rage so strong I felt myself tremble:

"What are we waiting for?"

I sensed the tension below. Everything depended on the orders Captain Warder brought back. Most of the men came up on deck.

We crowded the deck waiting for him. A few minutes after 9 a.m., a launch sped out toward us. The Skipper was in it. He carried a large white official-looking envelope in his hand, and I saw him limp slightly as he climbed over the rail. His knee was still bothering him. He turned to the coxswain who had helped him over. "Thank you," he said quietly, and went below. The officers followed him. I trailed behind. "Willie," I heard Captain Warder say, "what I want ..." And then: "We're going to take on more fish."

A moment later Sousa boomed the order to load stores and ammunition. We set to work. Another launch roared up from the *Canopus*. She carried torpedoes. We rigged our booms. The huge warheads began to swing over. More launches raced out to us from the *Canopus*, loaded to the gunwales with dry stores and fresh provisions. A hand-to-hand brigade was set up on deck, and as boxes were hauled up we passed them along and down into the hatches. Launches scurried back and forth over the waters of the bay, their wakes crisscrossing each other, supplying torpedoes to the submarines, food for their men. The entire crew of the *Wolf* worked like beavers. We stocked up on milk, canned ham, canned chicken, sacks of beans, sacks of coffee, sacks of rice. We had no room for fresh vegetables now. We began throwing overboard cans of paint, bright-work polish, and useless tools—everything not essential to the business of war. The *Wolf*'s spit-and-polish days were over.

We took lunch on the run—sandwiches, and coffee. Gus Wright, the cook, and our three Filipino messboys were all over the boat. As I stopped for a moment topside to gulp down my coffee, I could see Cavite's three giant radio towers piercing the blue sky. How long would they be standing there, I wondered? What messages were going out from them to the world right now? Just after lunch an oil lighter drew alongside. We loaded to capacity with fuel. Supper came at 7 p.m. Thick steak, french fried potatoes, asparagus, and ice cream. The crew was almost light-hearted now. "Let's get going!" you'd hear, and then a burst of swearing, and someone saying, "What are we waiting for? Time's awastin', ducks on the pond, let's be away!"

Thirty minutes later we were called to quarters. The skipper had a message for us. We lined up. Captain Warder, not much older than many of us, looked us over quietly. The smallest vestige of a smile was on his lips, but it was a grim smile. It was as though he were saying to us, without putting it into words, "Well, boys, here it is. You and I are going to be damn busy. It's serious as hell because it's war, but we're ready for it. We're the *Seawolf* and now we really begin the job we got to do."

What he said, was: "Men, we're leaving here tonight. We are escorting a convoy made up of the *Langley,* the oil tanker *Pecos,* and the U.S.S. *Black Hawk*. The *Sculpin* and the *Seawolf* will escort these ships south."

He paused. His left hand closed and opened and closed and opened again at his side—a habit of his when he was deeply moved. "Needless to say, you all know we're not playing any more. We're out after them now. Let's get them."

The *Wolf* left Manila at 10 p.m. The words on Captain Warder's orders were clear and precise: *"You will sink or destroy enemy shipping wherever encountered."*

We had no chance to cable our families that we were all right. We'd have to wait for that later—somewhere, somehow. We knew we had our work cut out. Philippine waters are dangerous for submarines. Coral reefs, treacherous rocks, shoals, and in many places little depth to maneuver in, all add up to trouble.

And the waters themselves are so clear that planes can easily spot submarines. We moved swiftly, but carefully, through the mine fields in Manila Bay, and then opened up to the best speed the surface ships could maintain. We were constantly on the alert. The night lookouts kept their eyes glued to their binoculars. Any moment we expected a wave of Jap bombers overhead. We strained every sense watching and listening for Jap submarines. We knew they must be racing toward us. News bulletins sputtered over the radio. The Japs had bombed Davao on the island of Mindanao. They had bombed Zamboanga on the southern tip of the Philippines. They'd landed on the north coast of Luzon. They'd bombed the important airfield at Aparri, 250 miles from Manila on the northeast tip of Luzon. They'd seized the International Settlement in Shanghai, bombed Hong Kong and even Singapore. Huge invasion forces had been sighted headed for the Philippines. Don Bell, the Manila news commentator, an honest, straight-from-the-shoulder broadcaster, was on the air without rest, giving additional details of the bombing of Pearl. And after Pearl, Cavite was their logical target .... But we saw the surface ships safely through the narrow and dangerous Verde Island passage south of Corregidor, and left them at dawn the next morning. As the sun rose on the ninth of December, we made our first day-long dive. We were on our first mission of the war; and from now on, unless we found ourselves in the safety of our own ports, the *Wolf* would never show more than her periscope in daylight.

My watches were 4 to 8 a.m. and 4 to 8 p.m., and at any other time of the day or night in emergency. As soon as my first watch was over, I stepped out into the control room. I wanted to know where we were headed. I asked the first man I saw—Chief Machinist's Mate Carl Enslin, a 200-pounder called "Swede," although he always insisted he was Pennsylvania Dutch. He was standing his watch as diving officer, his eye on the Christmas Tree.

"Don't you know?" he asked, surprised.

"I just came off watch," I explained. "I haven't heard a damn thing."

He pointed to the chart table. "It's all plotted out there," he said.

I squeezed past him to the small desk covered with charts of the Pacific waters. A thin red line had been drawn from Manila south through the San Bernardino Straits, up around the east coast of Luzon, up to the northeast point—to Aparri itself. We were going straight into the heart of hell. Aparri was under fire, the area was swarming with Jap ships, and it was the nearest point to Formosa.

"Oh, oh," I said. "We ought to see some business up there."

"We'll probably be in the thick of it in a couple of days," said Swede, keeping the Christmas Tree in view in the corner of his eye. As long as all the lights were green, all was well. A red light meant a hatch open somewhere.

I was due to get some sleep. I still wasn't altogether over my big head. I climbed up and threw myself in my bunk. We dressed for comfort on the *Wolf*—sandals, shorts, and undershirt—and I kicked off my sandals and lay down as I was and tried to sleep. But I was too geared up. The *Wolf*'s powerful electric motors kept up a steady, high-pitched whine, and I thought of Marjorie and Spike, and how worried Marjorie must be, and how I could get word to her that I was all right. I finally dozed off.

My second watch was nearly over that night when Don Bell's voice came in again. He said he was standing on the roof of the Manila Hotel.

"I have been here most of the day watching the methodical destruction of Cavite," he said. He sounded tired. "Right now Cavite is a mass of smoke and flame. The Japs have been very accurate today. There has been no opposition in the air. I have seen wave after wave of heavy bombers and dive bombers concentrate on Cavite. The destruction is complete. God knows how many men have been lost. The Japs haven't left the water front untouched, either. They have continuously bombed piers and water-front installations. So far they are leaving the ships in the harbor alone. They are probably waiting, knowing they will have plenty of time for that." And then a brief halt in his words. "Ladies and gentlemen, I don't know when I shall be back on the air, but I shall be back, God willing."

We had missed being caught by less than forty-eight hours. Later we learned that the *Dragon* got away safely, but the *Lion* was so badly damaged she had to be destroyed to prevent her falling into the enemy's hands.

My second watch over, I tried to sleep again. All at once someone was shaking me. "Eck! Eck! They want you in sound."

I jumped out of my bunk, ducked through the hatch and down the passageway to the sound shack. Maley was there, hands pressed over his phones. He shook his finger for silence and listened for ten seconds more. His face was strained.

"Here," he said, and pulled off the phones. "I can't figure it out, Eck. I got something here, and I don't know what in hell it is."

I sat down and took over. Maley stood by.

There was a soft chatter in the phones. Two detectors transmitting to each other, conversing with each other? Jap submarines? Our first contact of the war? I listened intently. I adjusted my dials to hair-like accuracy. I turned on the intercom system after a minute and reported:

"Captain, I have something on the sound gear that sounds like two Jap subs talking to each other."

"Give me a bearing, Eckberg," came back Captain Warder's voice.

I turned my wheel carefully, trying to find the point on 360-degree dial where the chatter was the loudest. I tried to pin it down to a definite spot in a definite direction from the *Wolf*, but I couldn't.

"They're all over the dial," I said. "I get them everywhere."

"Does it sound like the Japs?" he asked.

"Yes, sir."

Silence for a moment. Then the Skipper's voice, very calm: "Well, keep giving me information, Eckberg. Keep it up."

"Yes, sir," I said. I didn't like it. Submarines can ram each other underwater, and if one locates the other by sound, it can even send a torpedo after it. If two Jap subs were closing in on us from either side ... But if the sound did come from another submarine, the bearings must show a change over a period of time, and these did not. Since it was impossible for another submarine to be gliding alongside of us, at the same speed, at the same distance, never varying in angle, the noise must come from something else.

It might be caused by the water striking the coral reefs. That produces a whistling sound. Or by porpoises breaking the surface of the water. Yet, as I listened, Maley beside me, I knew it was none of these. I racked my brains. What were the peculiarities of these waters ... Suddenly I had it. *Reef fish!* Small, green-bellied "croakers" which emit a blubbering, bullfrog-like grunting under water that can deceive the most expert ear. I told it to Maley, and he grinned. I reported to the Captain, feeling a little sheepish.

"Fish, Eckberg?" Over the intercom came a chuckle. "Better go back and finish your sleep. You need it."

We surfaced as darkness fell. As soon as the hatch was opened, we started our Diesels to recharge batteries. Captain Warder, always the first man on the bridge when we surfaced, climbed up, and after him the Officer of the Deck, a duty taken in rotation by the officers. Then came the night lookouts; then the signalmen; later the mess cooks with the garbage of the last twenty-four hours, which they cast overboard. Of the sixty-five men in the *Wolf*, these were the only ones who went topside day or night without special permission. If more were permitted, a crash dive would catch them like rats. Groups of the men below crowded about the ladder, breathing deep gulps of the fresh air coming down from the bridge and sucked aft by the Diesels. The smell of baking bread came to me as I lay in my bunk. The cooks had begun their "hot cooking"—meats and fish and baking—because the odors could escape now, and the blowers were wafting these tantalizing smells into every compartment.

Maley took over the radio watch to receive and transcribe messages now that we could use our antenna. The sea was choppy and the *Wolf* rolled considerably. I was alternately asleep and awake, and finally gave up altogether, wandering into Kelly's Pool Room in time to hear a tinny jazz band playing "It's Three O'Clock in the Morning." It was Radio Tokyo, and Tokyo Rose was on. She was a female Lord Haw Haw who had sold out to the Japs, and she opened her program with old-fashioned sentimental songs. The idea, I suppose, was to make us homesick. She was taunting us now about Japanese victories and Allied defeats. She sunk the U.S. fleet as we listened, night after night. "Where is the great United States fleet?" she began in her phony Oxford accent. "I'll tell you where it is! It's lying at the bottom of Pearl Harbor." She went on to tell us all the details. Her voice rose hysterically:

"Why don't you give up, you fools out there? You can't stand up against the power of the Imperial Fleet!"

Some of the men were playing cards on the mess tables, two of the mess cooks were peeling potatoes, and our retorts were unprintable.

There were all sorts of stories about Tokyo Rose. One was that she was an Englishwoman who'd married a Jap. We listened; amazed at the statistics she reeled off to prove we were being licked. She gave names and tonnage of the ships she said we had lost, and the dates and the places. This might have worked on us after a while, if it weren't for John Street, a slow-spoken, casual, six-foot Machinist's Mate from Colorado. John loved figures. He liked to read them, write them, and add them up. A crack accountant was lost when he went into the Navy to take charge of No. 2 engine on the *Wolf*. He was always armed with the "book"—a combination dictionary and encyclopedia—and under his bunk he'd packed away *Jane's Fighting Ships*, the latest edition of the *World Almanac*, and a *Universal History* in one volume. Street would take out a carefully sharpened pencil, wet the point between his lips, and as Tokyo Rose cited the destruction of the American fleet, he took down the names of the ships. Then he looked them up. "She's all wrong," he'd say, mildly. "We didn't have that many ships in the fleet in the first place."

After she signed off we tuned in Station KGEI, the short-wave station in San Francisco. Now we heard the list of Jap ships the U.S. had sunk. John listened to this as carefully, and as methodically looked up the record. He said sadly, "Hell, there's no more navies left in the world." We knew the Frisco radio was broadcasting for Jap consumption.

Now the *Wolf* was moving cautiously. We were cruising off the northeastern coast of Luzon, off Aparri itself. The Japs had landed here within the last twenty-four hours. This was the spearhead of their attack, their toughest job. Luzon was more heavily protected than any other Philippine island, and the Japs had to take Luzon if they wanted a base for planes. They'd hit Aparri hard, roaring up to the beach in armored barges and streaming ashore by the thousands, falling in front of withering fire, yet pouring in until by sheer weight of numbers they gained a foothold. If we could get a crack at one of those transports ... If we could send a fish into the guts of one of those big babies ...

These were very dangerous waters. We dove at 4:30 a.m. I completed my morning watch at 8 a.m. and fell asleep in my bunk, in shorts and sandals this time. About an hour later I was awakened by a shout. Something on sound again! It looked as if I'd never catch up on sleep. I took over the sound shack. I searched. I sent up my message to the conning tower: "Sound has something, sir."

Lieut. Holden's deep voice came back: "Very well. Control, what's your depth?"

"Eighty-five feet, sir," came from the man at the depth gauge.

"Bring her up to periscope depth, and we'll have a look."

"Aye, aye, sir." The word was relayed to the bowplanesman:

"Bring her up and be careful. We may have something up there."

The *Wolf* rose silently through the dark waters.

"Here we are, sir," from the bowplanesman.

"Up periscope." Holden's voice was almost casual. We heard the drone of the periscope sliding upward in its channel. A moment later: "Down periscope!" Holden's voice had a new note in it. "Call the Captain."

A messenger hurried to Captain Warder's stateroom. In less than two minutes the Skipper, in shorts and sandals, was climbing up the ladder. His sandals made a slapping sound. His deliberate words came over the intercom: "What do you have, Mr. Holden?"

"A Jap destroyer, sir. Portside bearing three one zero relative."

"Good!" said Captain Warder. "Up periscope." He held it up there less than fifteen seconds. "Down periscope. Battle stations."

His voice had scarcely faded away before the raucous *aaaap! aaaap!* of the battle-station alarm blared through the boat. Half-naked, their bodies gleaming in the yellow light, the men tumbled out of their bunks. The narrow passageways were suddenly filled with men and then as suddenly cleared as each man fitted into his assigned position.

The approach party—the men who had to plot the maneuvering to place the *Wolf* in the best possible position to fire, taking into account her course and the enemy's course and speed—grouped themselves about the plotting table in the control room. They were Ensign Mercer, Ensign Casler, Frank Franz, and one H. H. Thompson, called "Hard-Hearted Henry" simply because of his initials. Maley hurried in to stay with me in sound. Rudy Gervais, an exuberant Frenchman, just twenty-one, his face shining, his dark brown eyes alert, took over as helmsman.

Everyone was at his post.

In sound, Maley and I, with our phones on, listened hard. As from a great distance, I heard a gentle *Ping! ... Ping!* as though someone had plucked the E string of a violin. This was the telltale sound of the enemy's sound-detection apparatus. He was searching for us—sending out electrical sound waves—and we were listening for him. We waited.

Over the intercom, Captain Warder's even voice: "She's a Jap, all right. Akasaki class. Big destroyer. Guns mounted fore and aft. Multiple torpedo tubes midships. Depth charge racks. Estimated course, zero seven zero. Estimated speed, fifteen knots. Range, 3,000 yards. Seems to be patrolling outside a cove." Pause. "Down periscope." Then, in a satisfied tone: "We'll wait a couple of minutes. Then we'll make another check."

Zero seven zero meant the enemy was on a course 70 degrees from true north. Zero zero one, for example, would mean one degree; three five nine would mean 359 degrees. Thus we could plot our approach, having the enemy's course from a fixed point on the horizon.

The crew of the *Wolf* waited, silent. Slowly we slipped into position. The sea was rough now; we rolled and pitched. I had the Jap propellers in my earphones: *whish—sh ... whish-sh ... whish-sh ...* and now and then a suddenly weakened *fluff ... fluff ... whish ... sh!* The enemy destroyer was pitching so heavily that every few seconds his propellers cleared the water altogether and churned the air.

"Ah!" Captain Warder's voice was eager. "She's heading directly for us. Probably en route to the homeland. We won't attack until we get in a more favorable position." Then a change in his voice: "Wait a minute, wait a minute! ... If the Japs have a destroyer out here, they must have something *inside* that cove." Silence. Then, as though debating with himself: "Sea conditions are against me. Fish might broach. On the other hand, this *is* a man-of-war. He's enemy shipping. I'm ordered out here to destroy him. But if I attack, successful or not, they'll know I'm here, and then they'll pull whatever they have inside that cove away from here."

The *Wolf* marked time. Captain Warder was thinking it through. Was it to be this Jap destroyer, sitting before us, a fat, inviting target, or was it wiser to ignore him and set our sights for bigger prizes inside the cove? Two full minutes dragged by. No one spoke. I heard men coughing, clearing their throats, shuffling, making the small noises men make under pressure. Deeper in the boat, men stood and watched the loud speakers, waiting. I heard the Jap's screws over sound. I spun my dials, kept him clear, and gave the Captain his bearings:

"Screws bearing zero two zero, Captain."

"Very well, Eckberg." Still preoccupied.

"Target seems to be drawing aft, Captain."

"Yes—ss, that's right. He's staying on the same course. Let me know if the pattern changes." Then, with sudden finality:

"Secure battle stations. We will not attack. We're going to look inside that cove."

The whole crew relaxed. But the tension was gone only momentarily. The *Wolf* was going into that cove and make the Japs like it, too. We'd see action quickly enough. Kelly's Pool Room became crowded with men off duty drinking coffee and talking things over. Captain Warder and Lieutenant Deragon pored over their charts in the control room: slim men both, one big, the other small, both in khaki shorts and sandals, their bodies glistening with perspiration under the subdued light. Circumspection was the word now.

All that day we patrolled carefully, waiting for cover of darkness. With nightfall, the seas grew mountainous. We drew away from the bay: Captain Warder wanted his men to catch some sleep during the night.

A few of us tried to doze off, but we were too tense. Some of the boys were seasick. Most of us stayed at our stations, checking and rechecking our gear. Langford and his torpedo crew toiled over their fish. It takes six strong men to move a torpedo on its rollers and bring it out for inspection. At Squeaky's command, the men seized a heavy line and tugged. The great, twenty-foot torpedo slid out on its tiny rollers from the loading rack. They went over it as a diamond cutter goes over his diamond, then slowly they slid it noiselessly back into place.

We submerged at dawn and started into the cove. The approach was a delicate matter. We spent four hours negotiating the short distance, making periscope observations every few minutes. The order would come, "Up periscope." The glistening metal pillar—for all the world like a huge, shining perpendicular piston—would glide up with a soft drone, up out of its well until the periscope lens was above the surface of the water, far overhead. Captain Warder would place both arms over the two crossbars protruding more than a foot from either side of the periscope base, and, half-hanging on them, his forehead pressed against the sponge-rubber eyepiece, he would rotate with it like some strange acrobat in slow motion. I knew what it was like to look through that eyepiece: the sense of shock you had when you saw the brightness of daylight, the sun sparkling on the blue waters of the sea. Looking through a periscope is like looking through a high-powered binoculars: almost under your nose the sea heaves and tosses, so near that you almost pull back from the spray. The droplets of water roll down with amazing speed from the elliptical object glass, and the image is framed and clear. If the sun were too bright, a twist of the wrist—and a green filter fell into place. I knew that with a flick of his right hand Captain Warder could reduce his magnification to 75 percent of normal— this if he found himself so near a target that it occupied the entire field of vision and a lesser magnification would give him a more complete picture of target and surroundings. With another flick of his hand he could sweep the sea from horizon to sky; a glance downward at the periscope base, and he knew almost instantly how far away, in yards, the target stood; and all these infinite calibrations could, with a single press of his right thumb, be transferred into the very torpedoes themselves so that, once fired, they became all but human flashing toward their victim at such a rate of speed, with such a change in direction, set to explode precisely at contact.

Slowly we crept up on our still-unseen prey. In the silence, above the steady whine of the *Wolf's* motors, we could hear overhead the gurgle and splash of the sea itself. The Skipper gave way, after a little while, to Lieutenant Holden, and with each "Up periscope" Holden took his navigation fixes, using points of land for reference. Stationed at sound, I heard the rough sea. The water noises were deafening, a roaring, snapping, crackling bedlam blaring through my phones like static in a terrific electrical storm. To hear the beating of a ship's screws above this scratching inferno of sound meant listening with such intensity that often you mistook the pulsations of your own blood for the enemy.

Suddenly Holden's deep voice rang out: "Call the Captain!"

The Skipper raced up the ladder. "What have you got, Mr. Holden?"

"I don't know, sir. I saw the mast of a ship."

"Can you make him out at all?"

"No, sir."

The Captain took over the periscope. He studied the sea for a full minute, then pulled the periscope down again. "There's a ship in there, all right. Looks like a big baby. *Hmmmm.*" Silence. "Mr. Mercer"—he was turning to Ensign Mercer, standing over his charts on a tiny desk less than three feet away—"how's the depth of that water?"

"We can't go in far, sir," said Mercer. His voice had a different timbre. "It's pretty shallow. But I think we can get within firing range."

"Good!" said the Captain. "Up periscope." A moment later: "Jap seaplane tender at anchor. Looks about 12,000 tons ..."

Down below, in the sound room, Maley and I looked at each other.

"Seaplane tender!" Maley pursed his lips in a silent whistle. "Now wouldn't that make a nice Christmas present for the boys!"

Captain Warder's voice was even. "Bearing three five five relative. Guns fore and aft. Two stick mast cranes. Might be a sub tender. Something alongside of her that might be subs or seaplanes. Down periscope."

Maley scratched his head. "Funny we don't patrol in a little closer."

"Hell," I said, "there's that Nip destroyer right around the corner. He can get here in ten minutes."

Maley looked at me almost scornfully. He was young, and he wanted action. "He won't help her if we get her first, will he? Let's sink the damn thing now and worry about him later."

I said nothing. Silence in the conning tower. I had a pretty clear idea of what was taking place up there. Captain Warder, brows knit, was at his chart desk, checking carefully through his confidential papers, trying to type the Jap ship we wanted to attack. Apparently he was satisfied, for a minute later:

"Battle stations!" sang out the tinny voice of the intercom.

"Battle stations!" echoed from bow to stern of the *Wolf*. Before the words died out, the *aaap! aaaap! aaaaap!* of the battle alarm rang through the boat.

The emergency lights were snapped on. A dull reddish glow suffused the interior of the *Wolf*.

"Up periscope ... Make ready the bow tubes. Down periscope."

Behind the Captain, Signalman Frank Franz stood with phones and chest telephone. He was the Captain's talker and relayed his orders. He repeated: "Forward torpedo room, make ready the bow tubes."

The *Wolf* slowed down so that when her periscope was raised again she would not cause a noticeable wave.

"Open outer doors," ordered Captain Warder.

Talker repeated: "Open outer doors."

In the control room below a man worked feverishly spinning a huge control wheel by hand ... ten revolutions, eleven, twelve, thirteen, fourteen ... Far forward in the bow, two great steel doors in the *Wolf*'s hull swung slowly open, exposing the blunt heads of the torpedoes ...

"Forward tubes ready, Captain," Franz reported. "Outer doors open."

"Up periscope!" said the Skipper. A few moments later: "Stand by."

Then: "No, no, wait a minute! Rudy, come left a little more, little more ... there! Hold her, Rudy... Fire one!"

There was a sudden *whoosh!* as though the safety valve of a radiator had blown off. Then a gentle kickback, as though the *Wolf* coughed, suddenly alive. I felt the pressure on my eardrums.

Torpedoes are fired by an impulse of compressed air. The air pressure within the boat goes up correspondingly.

The crew was on its toes: water had to be flooded into tanks to compensate for the change in the boat's weight and center of gravity. The *Wolf* had to be trimmed, placed in balance again, or she might bounce to the surface like a rubber ball.

On the phones I picked up the sound of the torpedo, a high-pitched whine as she tore through the water. Captain Warder, I knew, had his eyes glued to the periscope. His orders came crisply.

"Stand by to fire two ... Fire two!"

Again the hiss, the jar, the gentle kickback, again and again.

As each fish left, I picked it up on sound. The first whine died out, then the second came into my phones. It died out. I waited tensely for the explosions. The skipper kept his eyes glued to the periscope. I listened hard. I had to keep my ears on those torpedoes. An erratic fish can circle about and come back to blow you into Kingdom Come.

Captain Warder's voice was sharp: "I can see them .... *They're running hot* ... Jesus! They missed the target! Oh, hell! Make ready the aftertubes. Open outer doors in after-room! Hard right rudder!"

He ordered the *Wolf* full speed ahead. "All ahead, full! Eckberg, hear those fish run?"

Yes, I had heard them run. But I'd also heard dull thuds. They were like knife thrusts into my heart. I knew what had happened. The torpedoes had missed the target, continued on, and exploded on the beach.

I reported heavily. "Yes, sir. All ran hot and missed the target."

"Hmmmm," said the Captain. Then: "Rudy, come to course two seven zero. Let me know when you get there. Sound, do you hear any propellers?"

I searched intently. "No screws, sir."

"Good!" said the Skipper. He was as disappointed as a man can be, but he hadn't given up hope yet.

Rudy's voice came over the intercom: "Steady on course two seven zero, sir."

"Very well, all ahead one-third," replied the Captain.

"One-third, sir," said Rudy.

The *Wolf*, her speed reduced to one-third, moved slowly forward.

The Captain said: "Up periscope. Are the after tubes ready? Okay. There's a lot of activity up here, as far as I can see. They are trying to get under way. Come right a little, Rudy ... Hold it there, Rudy .... Stand by to fire .... Fire!"

Again I picked up the high, thin whine of the fish.

"Easy now, Rudy ... Close the outer doors ... All ahead, standard. I see him now.... They're running straight again—"

I was listening to the fish with all my ears. They were running straight and hot, all right. Then *ka-boom!* The *Wolf* shuddered. Then again, and again, and again. This time our torpedoes had run straight and home. The concussion shook us each time.

"Explosions, Captain!" I barked into the mike.

"I can see her!" he snapped back. "Wait ... wait ... They may have hit in the bow." Then, eagerly: "I see white water. I see a lot of white water! Down periscope!"

We dared expose our periscope no longer. There was a murmur of conversation between the Skipper and Ensign Mercer. Captain Warder, we learned later, wasn't sure if our fish struck the Jap or not. The crew to a man was certain that at least one had hit. But Captain Warder did not even claim this ship as damaged. He had not seen it go down. He was not positive.

"Proceed with the reloads," he finally ordered. "We are expecting company any minute. Keep careful watch, sound." Then, a moment later: "Send Mr. Syverson up, please."

In a few minutes the Skipper was talking to Ensign Donald Syverson, torpedo officer, a stubby, red-headed, personable sub man from Michigan.

"I can't understand it," the Captain said quickly. "I don't know what was wrong with those first fish. Got any ideas about it?"

"No, sir." Syverson sounded crestfallen. "We readied them according to instructions, Captain. I inspected them myself."

"I can't figure it out," said the Skipper, musingly.

I began hearing telltale sounds again. *Ping! ... ping ... ping!*

"Got a ship up there, Captain," I announced.

"Propellers or pings, Eckberg?"

"Pings, Captain. I think they're on the starboard side, well aft."

"What do you mean, they? More than one?"

"Yes, sir. I hear two of them."

We waited. And then, far distant, a muffled boom! The *Wolf* shook. Her joints creaked. The lights flickered, went out for a moment, then on again. It was a depth charge, mild because it was some distance away. Actually, no depth charge attack can be called mild, because when 700 or 800 pounds of TNT explode in your general vicinity, any number of things can happen. A depth charge doesn't have to score a direct hit to sink you. Water is incompressible. An explosion can write your finish if it's near enough for the concussion to place sufficient pressure on the water surrounding your boat to stave it in or crush it altogether.

The exploding charges were something special to hear. They sounded as though a giant smashed together boulders as large as houses under the water with pulverizing force. If you've ever heard two stones struck together under water, you know how booming and terrifying that small report can sound, intensified and expanded by the water. But this charge, and the one or two that followed, were too far away to harm us. And after a while, there were no, more explosions and no more pings.

"Hear any propellers about?" asked the Skipper. I said no, and he ordered the boat taken to the regular diving depth. We cruised back into rough water; water so rough I could hear the choppy waves rippling the surface of the sea. A few minutes later, Captain Warder ordered the periscope up again. He spent five long minutes scanning the water.

"Hell, it's black up here tonight," he murmured. "Damn rough, too. There's a fire near the beach. That might be one of our ships burning. It's so black up here I can't see the land at all.... Well, we'll head out to open sea and charge batteries."

For some nights and days we made routine patrols, and then one night we began one of the most dangerous tasks a submarine can undertake in wartime— relocating our torpedoes. The *Wolf* had space on deck to stow extra torpedoes. Since these are massive weapons, relocating them—moving them from the deck to the torpedo rooms below—is a sizable job. Booms must be rigged, loading hatches must be opened, and the submarine is exposed to any attack. Her men are topside, live torpedoes are dangling from the booms, hatches are open, and a crash dive is impossible. Here, particularly, with Jap land all about us, we'd be a sitting duck for the first plane or destroyer to sight us.

The Skipper took every precaution. While he scanned his charts in the control room, the four men who were to take over the bridge lookouts when we surfaced lounged in the mess hall reading magazines through infrared glasses, preparing their eyes for the darkness above. Captain Warder finally decided to surface in the lee of a small island. The brassy, harsh surface horn jangled. The *Wolf* slowly rose.

"Open the hatch," the Skipper ordered.

The toggle-bolts were whirled loose, the hatch was pushed open. There was a rush of air like a small gale sweeping past us.

The *Seawolf* bobbed gently on the surface of the sea.

Word came from topside that a radio insulator—one of the two on which my antenna was strung—was smashed. I asked permission to go topside and fix it.

"I don't know, Eckberg," Captain Warder said dubiously, rubbing his chin. "We're not in a healthy place. They can ram us or shell us before we can get down. The less people I have on the bridge, the better I like it."

But our antenna might snap, I said, and I could fix it in a couple of minutes. Okay, he said, go ahead—but fast. I climbed up the ladder and out into God's fresh air. The clouds had vanished, and now the night was perfect. The full moon, bright as a new penny, flooded the ocean with its light. The high seas had died down; the water was calm, with only the gentlest swell running. I took a deep breath and tasted the heavy salt air. It was so heavy I felt dizzy. I could see the thin outline of a small island less than half a mile away. I breathed deeply again. I couldn't get enough fresh air into my lungs. This was the first time since Manila that I had been topside, under the sky. It seemed a long time then, but I was to learn that it was nothing compared to what was in store for us later.

The insulator was easily fixed, and when I climbed down again, half a dozen of the crew were crowded about the foot of the ladder trying to get as near the fresh air as they could.

"It had to be you who went up, didn't it?" complained Maley. "Goddammit, I'd give my right arm to be able to take a ten-minute walk in a park now."

I slapped him on the back. "Nothing like fresh air to put pep into a man," I said. I made it back into the sound room with a string of catcalls following me.

We finished relocating torpedoes and our battery charging. Now that we were on the surface, I set the radio to intercept instructions from the High Command. Messages began to pour into my phones. As fast as I copied them down, a messenger took them up to the Skipper to decode in the wardroom. We learned then that we were the first submarine to come out of the Philippines, and that our attack on the seaplane tender had been the first U.S. submarine attack of World War II.

All that night we remained in the open sea. Before dawn we dove and started back to the beach where we had made our first attack. The Skipper wanted to look for ships. We went in the same entrance and arrived at the same point where we had fired our torpedoes. I heard the Skipper at the periscope:

"I'll never find out if I sunk that bastard or not. After the war is over I'll come up here again and investigate."

The sea turned rough and dirty. Waves as big as housetops were breaking on the surface, and I heard their steady rumbling on sound. That night we again returned to the open sea and recharged batteries. Two nights later we received a radio report of the War Department's announcement: a flotilla of transports estimated to include many thousands of Japanese soldiers was moving into the Lingayen Gulf, escorted by planes and destroyers. And that night Wake Island fell. We knew Wake couldn't hold out indefinitely, but were encouraged to think how long a handful of Marines could tell the Japs to go to hell.

We received orders to return to Cavite. The Japs had thrown a cordon of warships around the entire Philippine area. Japanese warships were working with Japanese reconnaissance planes, and Tokyo had actually set up a chain of ships from Corregidor to Zamboanga, on the southern tip of the Philippines, ships so spaced that no surface unit could penetrate without being seen. Two out of every three Allied ships that tried to run the blockade were sunk before they reached Manila Bay. We had to proceed with utmost caution. We turned homeward and began running south as we had run north—surfaced at night, submerged at day. The Japs were working fast. They'd moved close to Manila now, and everything that could be, had been moved to Corregidor.

Meanwhile, life had been going on as usual within the *Wolf.*

We had our jobs to do, and we did them. Off duty, there were long bullsessions and games of cribbage in Kelly's Pool Room. We discussed everything from religion to Walter Winchell. Most of us admired his courage in coming out with what he thought, but what got our fancy was how he predicted blessed events. "That guy must walk around with a keyhole," Zerk claimed. Men lay in their bunks reading magazines. Nearly all of us subscribed to the popular ones—the *Reader's Digest, Saturday Evening Post, Collier's, Liberty*—and to half a dozen colored comic magazines, and we got them regularly at Manila.

There wasn't much we could do about celebrating Christmas, but we had our little surprise, anyway. The first inkling I had was when I strolled into the mess hall after my afternoon watch on December 24 and began reading an article on air power by Alexander de Seversky. At that moment Sully, who'd seemed pretty busy the last few days, walked in. His red face was beaming. He rubbed his hands. He looked at me reading my magazine, at Sousa, who was flipping through a deck of cards, at Zerk, thumbing moodily through an old *Esquire,* and he said: "Well, boys, she's finished. Want to take a look at her?"

"What's finished?" I asked. Now, if it was something special in a cake he'd been laboring on ...

"Why, my Christmas tree," said Sully. "Want to see it?"

Sousa looked up from his cards. "By God, it *is* Christmas Eve, come to think of it!"

Zerk hitched up his trousers. "That's right," he said, as though this was the first time he had thought about it, too.

Sully was annoyed. "Do you or don't you want to see the damn thing?" he demanded.

We followed Sully into the forward battery and into the yeoman's office, and there on nice green monk's-cloth he'd set it up—his Christmas tree. It was a beautiful job. Coming down from Aparri he'd begun it. He'd started with a broom handle, drilled holes in it, then borrowed a handful of applicator sticks from Loaiza and inserted them into the holes. They became the branches. Then he'd got some red and blue flag bunting from Frank Franz. He'd made tinsel by gluing tinfoil from cigarette packages to strips of paper, and decorated the branches with that. He'd painted half a dozen flashlight bulbs green and red and silver and strung them about on a dry-battery circuit, and so his Christmas tree gleamed green, red, and silver—a work of art two feet high.

For the next twenty minutes a steady stream of men came to see and admire. Even Zerk admired it. "But it needs presents," he said.

"Yeah," admitted Sully, and his face fell. "I couldn't bum those, though I bummed everything else."

Captain Warder looked in from his stateroom a few feet away.

"What's the excitement?" he asked.

"Take a look in here, Captain, if you want to see something pretty," I said. Everyone moved aside so he could see the tree.

"My, my," he said. He cocked his head to one side. "That certainly looks like the real thing. Who made it?"

Everyone looked at Sully. The red began to creep up his solid Irish face. "Aw," he said finally, "four or five of us made it, Captain. I did the constructing, but I bummed stuff all over the boat."

Then, suddenly encouraged: "Captain, is it all right if I take a picture of it?"

"Sure," said Captain Warder, grinning. "We don't want to miss that. Make some good ones while you're at it."

For the next ten minutes Sully perspired. He spread cotton batting about the base of the tree for snow. He made a little fireplace out of cardboard and stuck that behind the tree. He dashed to his bunk and came back with flood lights and camera, shouting directions. I had to hold a spot here; Zerk had to hold another there.

"For Christ sakes, Eck, keep your face out of this," he shouted. "This is going to be pretty."

He was standing up, crouching, sighting along his nose—the perfect picture of the demon stage director. Even Captain Warder got into the picture, sitting down at one side of the table, smiling, his hair neatly brushed to one side. Then half a dozen other fellows posed with the tree.

We liked that little Christmas tree. The men would look at it, and someone would say, "Jeez, isn't that a pretty little thing," and then you'd hear someone else's voice, "Sure wish I was home tonight."

Zerk and I walked back slowly to the control room. On the way we met John Street, laughing like a madman.

"What's tickling you?" Zerk asked.

Street pointed to the after-engine room. We went in there. The noise of the Diesels was terrific, but everybody was standing around with pleased smiles. I went up to the nearest man standing at the throttle of No. 3 engine. I got right up to his ear.

"What tickled John Street so?" I yelled.

He pointed, too. I turned around, and there were two immense socks, four feet long. The foot alone was eighteen inches. One was bright red, the other white. They were made of bunting, and in those socks was the wildest collection of junk I'd ever seen in my life. A bunch of garlic; a twelve-inch Stilsen wrench; a can of oil; a pair of pink silk panties someone had got on some expedition of conquest; and on the socks were two Christmas tags.

One read, "From Mac to Snyder: Merry Christmas, I love you."

The other read: "From Snyder to McCoy: Best Wishes for Continued Prosperity and Good Luck in the Coming Year. Be glad when you're dead, you rascal, you."

We got a kick out of that. When we finally got into the control room, for no reason at all Manila jumped into my head, and I said, "I wonder how many of the boats got out of Manila."

Zerk, the supreme pessimist, sucked his pipe. "Damn few," he said.

I bristled. Perhaps it was homesickness after the Christmas tree, or impatience, but I stood up and snapped at him. "For Christ sakes, you're such a crepe-hanger somebody ought to punch you right in the face."

Zerk looked up and grinned. "Well, that's the way I see it," he said.

I stomped out. I felt low. I went into the galley and poured myself a big mug of hot coffee. I sat over it and began thinking. We were doing all right. This first mission of ours was damn important from more than one point of view. Here were the Japs, oozing confidence out of every pore, completely sold on the plans of their High Command, converging on a dozen different points; and where they found opposition they swiftly overwhelmed it.

They were coming down, step by step, clutching at everything within reach, eager for the petroleum-rich lands below them. The *Wolf*'s first attack served notice to the Jap fleet that the United States wasn't entirely caught off guard. Some units of the Asiatic Submarine fleet were still operating. The Japs simply couldn't cruise into any cove or harbor and think themselves completely safe from us. We were around. And because we *were* around, and because they now *knew* we were around, they dared not send unescorted merchant shipping over unprotected sea lanes. They'd have to pull warships off important jobs and assign them to convoy duty. We were doing fine. What was I glum about?

It was nearly midnight now, and I should have hit the sack, but I still didn't feel like sleep. Men were dropping into the galley, into Kelly's Pool Room, and everybody I passed on the way out was saying, "Merry Christmas." That warmed me up still more. I looked in on the radio shack. Snyder and Maley were in there, Snyder with the phones on, Maley bent over a book. Snyder saw me. He pushed his phones off his ears and said, "It's sure noisy around here. I don't know if I got anything here or not."

"Why don't you go aft and get some coffee?" I said. "I'll take over." He went out, and I slipped on the phones. Maley looked up, grunted, and went back to his reading.

It *was* noisy. We were close to shore, and I could hear the soft roar of the surf rolling up the beach. I listened hard. A distant, continuous echoing roar, like a seashell at your ear: that was the sound from the minute animal life clinging to the *Seawolf*'s keel. And then a backyard-like chattering—the merged sound of fish whistling, croaking, sighing. All these were the familiar sounds of the sea. I heard nothing suspicious.

I pushed off one earphone and turned to Maley. "Merry Christmas, kid," I said. He looked up and smiled. "Merry Christmas, Eck," he said, and went back to his reading.

Outside I heard the voice of Swede Enslin, "Merry Christmas, Mr. Deragon," and then our exec's mild, "Same to you, Swede."

There was a lump in my throat. I had to swallow a few times, sitting there, thinking, *Here it is Christmas, and Marjorie and Spike alone at home, not knowing if I'm dead or alive, and we're off Corregidor, and men are dying in Bataan, and we don't know if we're going to be dead or alive ourselves twenty-four hours from now ...*

Maley started to whistle softly. He had a gift for whistling. I sat there listening with one ear, my other tuned to the familiar sounds of the water, and all at once I felt better. Maley whistled pretty notes; he trilled like a bird. Well, it was Christmas. Marjorie and the little fellow were O.K. They were in a good home; they had enough food and heat. I wondered what they were doing this very minute. I'd sent her some beautiful things I'd picked up—raw silk, bolts of cloth, even a Mohammedan kriss, to decorate our home. Did the ship carrying those gifts ever get through?

I heard a man's heavy tread. It was Snyder.

"Okay, Eck," he said. "I'm ready to take over."

I took off the earphones. "Nothing to worry about on the gear, Snyder," I said, and I went forward and went to sleep.

There was a surprise Christmas Day. Gus Wright came into the mess hall and announced what we'd have for dinner that night—mince pies. He'd been up all night baking them, twenty of them. Gus was the hero of the boat that day. He was a thin fellow, about twenty-eight, with buck teeth and a pleasant way about him; and the fuss the crew made over his surprise made him so happy that his eyes got watery, and he went back into the galley and banged his pans around until he got it out of him. A Christmas tree, mince pies—well, it was a better Christmas than the boys had on Bataan and Corregidor, we thought.

All went smoothly aboard the *Wolf* until we approached south of Subic Bay, around 11 p.m. the night of the twenty-sixth. I began hearing pings. Captain Warder scoured the sea and horizon with his binoculars. Visibility was practically unlimited. A bright moon shone.

"I don't see a damn thing," he said.

But these pings could come from a Jap sub concealed under water, and we'd be silhouetted against the moon. We dove. When the moon set, we surfaced with infinite care and inched our way forward. At a point several miles off Corregidor, we picked up a small signal light. It was pointed toward us, blinking on and off, somewhere on the pitch-black shore. Someone was sending to us.

Frank Franz raced to the bridge and replied with our blinker gun, a tube-like instrument with a powerful light in it which can be aimed directly at a point

44

miles away and can't be seen at the right or left of the point. We established contact with the shore.

The message came through. A pilot was coming out in a FT boat to escort us through the heavily mined harbor.

A few minutes before midnight the PT boat suddenly emerged out of the darkness and unloaded a soft-spoken young man. He joined the Skipper on the bridge. The motors began to hum. I knew by the feel of the boat answering the rudder that we were going through the mine field, moving with infinite care toward the harbor. Then the *Wolf* halted; we had Mariveles Harbor on our port beam. The pilot left us.

Just before dawn, we pushed on again, heading farther into Manila Bay. The Skipper had orders to submerge there at a specified point. We finally found it and went down.

We marked time. Now and then a faint pounding came to our ears, as though someone were hammering on the hull of the *Wolf.* You couldn't mistake that sound. *The Japs were bombing Manila.* These were the explosions of their bombs coming down to us through the water. We listened, frustrated and impotent. We had little or no air support left in the Philippines then, and it wasn't pleasant knowing that our own men were being bombed on the surface and that we couldn't help them.

We surfaced at dusk and ran awash. We made a small target, difficult to observe. At 7 p.m. a message came over my radio ordering us into Corregidor. Captain Warder looked around.

"There's a ship out there," he said slowly. "She's burning."

We finally glided alongside the dock. We tied up. I received permission to secure the sound gear and some topside. I scrambled up the ladder and out the hatch. A shadowy figure grabbed my arm. It was the deck watch.

"Don't wander off too far," he warned me. "They're expecting an air raid."

I walked over the gangplank and stepped upon the dock of Corregidor.

CHAPTER III

We Take the High Command

IT WAS a perfect tropical night, with just a touch of chill in the air. The sky hung far above, strangely blue in the velvet darkness. The air seemed perfumed after the days and nights below. Off to my right was a dark blob of hilly land. That was Corregidor. Not a light shone. The shore was completely blacked out. Somewhere back there were General Douglas MacArthur and his ranking officers, mapping their defense against the Japs. The center of things had become Corregidor now: Manila was no longer in the picture. Standing there, breathing deeply, thinking about all the historic things that were being done all around me, I suddenly became conscious of a steady drone. For a moment I thought the enemy planes had come.

Then I realized that heavy trucks were plying back and forth on a sandy road which wound by the dock. A huge black shape low in the water caught my eye. I hadn't even seen it before: it was another submarine, the *Swordfish*. I recognized her large periscope shear braces. On her shakedown cruise, her assembly periscopes and radio masts vibrated so badly they had to build the braces to support them.

I lit a cigarette, cupping my hands to shield the flare, and walked slowly back and forth, breathing deeply. If only there were a way for me to get word to Marjorie that I was all right!

Of course, there was a radio here on Corregidor, but it could be used for military purposes only. Personal matters, no matter how urgent, had to wait. We had no idea where the *Wolf* was going after Corregidor. We might be out to sea for weeks on a patrol, and never once touch a point from which we could send a message to the States. How long would Marjorie have to undergo the ordeal of uncertainty?

The *Wolf*'s patrols, her comings and goings, were absolutely secret. Nothing could have been printed in the newspapers in the States, I knew. I pictured Marjorie telephoning the submarine base at New London, at Portsmouth, sending frantic wires to Washington. Months later, as a matter of fact, I learned that she did everything she could to learn about me. She told me she telephoned Washington and pleaded, "Just tell me if the *Seawolf* is safe. That's all I want to know. I want to know if my husband is alive."

They told her, "We're sorry, Mrs. Eckberg. Frankly, we don't even know where the *Seawolf* is. Things are breaking so fast I don't think anyone but President Roosevelt or Secretary Knox could tell you where any submarine is at any given moment now. You'll just have to wait."

The trucks were still going by, raising a slow dust which hung in the air like fog. The *Seawolf* was recharging her batteries. The heavy, nauseous fumes, blue-gray in the darkness, poured out of her exhaust pipes.

Suddenly, someone hit me a terrific blow on the back. I wheeled around. A giant of a man was standing there. In the darkness I peered up into his face.

"Eck, you red-headed son-of-a-gun, how in hell are you!"

Then I recognized him. It was Bull Kiser from 'Frisco, a radioman on the *Swordfish*. I'd gotten drunk with him in different parts of the world more times than I could remember. He was one of the strongest men I knew. His fingers were so large that when he'd punch a typewriter key, two letters jumped up.

So there, on the wooden dock at Corregidor, we thumped each other on the back and shook hands and talked over things. The *Swordfish* had been doing all right, he said.

"But we can't ever stick around to see whether they go down," he complained.

Like the *Wolf*, she had been attacking Jap men-of-war, and it was unhealthy to hang around after an attack to check up.

"We had plenty of close calls," he said.

He was not underrating the Japs, either. They were strong, they were treacherous, they weren't anything to laugh off too quickly. But we both agreed that the fact that we'd been able to re-enter Manila Harbor would prove to the Japs that their surface blockade couldn't keep us from coming in and going out as we liked. That would be bad medicine for those hissers to swallow.

By this time we had to get back to our boats. We shook hands. I never saw him again.

Quite a talkfest was filling the air in Kelly's Pool Room when I climbed down. Maurice ("Red") Jenkins, Chief Machinist's Mate, who came from Ohio and could make dice turn somersaults, wanted to know what in the name of Mary were we going to do now. Pop Rosario, the Filipino messboy, whose wife and children were, as far as he knew, dead at the hands of the Japs, would have been happy to climb out on the dock and meet the Japs hand to hand when they finally closed in. Where were we going now? Everyone guessed and nobody knew. Why had they brought us into Corregidor again? What was our next job?

That night we heard Tokyo Rose call for the surrender of the men on Bataan. "You are encircled," she cried. "You can give up now without dishonor."

"_____, _____," someone said precisely and profanely. We laughed.

At dawn the *Wolf* went out to sea again and submerged. Once more we heard the dull *rap! rap!* of Jap planes dive-bombing our shipping in Manila Harbor. We thought, "Well, hell, General MacArthur isn't going to let them get away with that too long! He'll get even, all right. We don't have to worry about that."

At dusk we surfaced and came into the same dock as before. Now we set to work in earnest. There were stores to load, and we worked without rest. Apparently we were going out that same day, and we weren't going out on a picnic. The sun rises in that latitude about 5 a.m., and we had to work fast if we wanted to get outside the mine, field while it was still dark, and remain on the surface and still be fairly well hidden from the Japs. By midnight oil lines had been hooked up to the *Wolf*, and hundreds of gallons were flowing into our tanks. We worked like stevedores bringing the endless stores aboard. The highly secret and confidential papers and other invaluable data were stowed in a safe position. I helped with the fuel line, and I carried boxes aboard. I looked over my radio gear, checking and rechecking it.

About an hour before midnight, as I was working in the sound room, Gunner Bennett stuck his head in. He had four yellow rectangular cans in his hands. I thought they were candy, at first—cans of hard candy.

"You know what these are, Eck?" said Gunner. "Dynamite." And before I was able to bounce back from that news, he said, "Here's the dope. Plant these. If we have to, before this ship is captured or abandoned, we got to destroy all gear that might help the Nips. That includes your radio and sound gear."

He gave me the cans, and I took them gingerly. Then he stuck his hand in his pocket and brought out four fuses, about five feet long. "These are slow-burning," he said. "But if you have to set them"—he grinned—"it won't matter if you get out of here fast or not. You won't be going nowhere."

We both laughed. I didn't think it was a very funny joke, and neither did Gunner. I stowed the dynamite into one of the lockers in the sound room and forgot about it.

At midnight the intercom coughed and announced "Deck force on deck. Others remain below. We are pulling out in a few minutes."

As I crossed through the control room on my way to the radio shack, I saw a man's legs coming down the conning tower ladder.

Life on a sub is so intimate that you instantly recognize your crewmates from any angle of vision you see them, and whether they are nude or fully dressed, walking away from you or coming toward you. These legs were strangers. And whoever it was, he was wearing big brown Army regulation shoes—something none of us wore on the *Wolf*. Then a pair of khaki trousers; and finally the rest of the stranger. He wore a tan field jacket; he turned, and I glimpsed a staggering amount of gold braid on the visor of his cap. Then I recognized him from photographs I'd seen. It was Captain James Fife, Jr., one of the highest submarine command officers in the United States Navy. Later he became Chief of Staff, Submarines, Asiatic Fleet, and received the Distinguished Service Medal. A broad-shouldered, rugged sea veteran, he looked around, his practiced eye taking in the *Seawolf*'s control room in one approving glance, nodded a courteous "good day" to me, and strode to the charts and began studying them.

More legs—strange legs—began to come down the ladder. This pair was the skinniest pair of shanks I had ever seen. Then bare knees; then a pair of shorts, and then the entire figure came into view, crowned with a white pith helmet. This, I learned later, was Major Wilkinson, aide to General Wavell.

All sorts of scuttlebutt ran through the boat now. It seemed we were taking the U.S. Submarine High Command out from Corregidor. The *Swordfish* would take out other members of the staff. Among those who left Corregidor at that time, we learned later, were Admiral Hart, Rear Admiral William Glassford, and other ranking U.S. officers.

With our visitors came two radiomen, Don Irish and Duke Woodard. Don, a tall, red-headed fellow about thirty, was gaunt and emaciated after his ordeal on the Rock. It took him days to fill out and regain his vitality. Woodard was thin, too, and suffered intensely from an ulcerated leg wound. Loaiza took him over, and I didn't see much of him until later. Don told me how they fought to keep their radio going on Corregidor, and gave me another picture of the doggedness and determination of the men who held out so long and so bravely against the Japs.

When they were ready to transmit, he said, four volunteers dashed out with a reel of wire, strung it over scrub brush, and rushed back to send their messages. Seconds later, Jap bombers roared over and blew the antenna to shreds. Undaunted, the Americans watched their chance, raced out again from their tunnel, and strung up a new antenna. And again the Japs rained fire and death from the air to destroy it. Yet, in the midst of that furious and ceaseless barrage, the boys strung up their antenna, sent their messages out, and kept the world informed of what they were doing. Food was a real problem, Don said. They ate only two meals a day, and most of each meal was rice. Their water supply was low. Their ammunition supply was low. Don couldn't give enough credit to the anti-aircraft batteries, who ran up records for shooting Jap planes out of the sky. The Americans had a delaying job to do, and they did it.

Captain Fife, having gone to the charts, virtually lived with them. He rarely came through the boat. The wardroom was crowded twenty-four hours a day. The messboys had to set up three eating shifts to accommodate everyone: three breakfasts, three lunches, three dinners—the cooks worked marvels preparing meals for more than eighty men on their tiny stove. They and the Filipino boys were real soldiers on the trip out. They never grumbled, yet they were continuously preparing food, serving food, removing food, setting dishes, washing dishes—and, in between, filling and refilling the ten-gallon coffee urn. An average submarine crew can drink thirty gallons of coffee every twenty-four hours—and more when it's under tension.

Bit by bit the word had been going through the boat that we were heading for Australia, taking the High Command there. That was a short trip—we'd be there in a few days.

Australia meant cable facilities and our first chance to let our folks back home know we were safe. The first moment I had I sat down at my desk and began composing one cable after another to Marjorie, trying to find words to explain all I wanted to say: how I felt when I couldn't reach her, how I knew she must have worried, how much I missed her and Spike, how I had their photographs right here in front of me when I worked and above my bunk when I slept, so that I saw them the last minute before I fell asleep and the first moment I awoke every morning. At last I settled on: "Feeling fine don't worry love to all." I had it neatly typed, with address and signature, and folded in my pocket days before we reached Australia.

Some of the crew asked Paul and me to help them with their cables. They crowded into the shack—it held only two persons besides us—and stood outside it and joked about what they'd send. We all felt a little embarrassed at showing our feelings. Zerk, sarcastic as always, would wander in and listen, and wander out again, but we took his ribbing without getting angry. He never received mail. He didn't know whether his wife and children were alive. When we used to reach port, before Pearl Harbor, and the mail pouch was thrown from the barge and the letters distributed, he'd find himself a stool somewhere and read a detective story.

On the way in both officers and crew of the *Wolf* were pretty satisfied with themselves. We'd have preferred action to evacuating personnel, but we realized that this was a mission comparable in importance to sinking enemy ships. After all, ships can be replaced, but submarine officers with the training of our passengers could not. And we were proving again that a surface blockade couldn't stop the *Wolf*. We were proving that the submarine has an advantage over all other craft because she could disappear from sight. No matter how well-spaced enemy units were, no matter how expertly set up to intercept submarines, the submarines could still be sailed through at fairly high speeds, covering great distances without undue strain on any member of the crew, its officers, or its passengers.

We were less than twenty-four hours out of Australia when the bridge lookout, about 1,500 hours, shouted: "Seaplane above the port bow!"

The alarm sounded. We rushed to battle stations. We flashed our recognition signals to the plane. The pilot flashed his—and for the next few minutes we had a bad time of it. Our signals didn't jibe.

If a pilot doesn't receive the correct signal, he drops his bombs first and investigates later. We could try to shoot him down. It would be a smaller loss to knock out one plane than to let a plane sink a submarine. But if we ordered the crew to their guns, the pilot might take that as a hostile act, and bomb us. All submarines look alike. If we did nothing, he might bomb us anyway.

It was a ticklish situation. Captain Warder thought it through—and did nothing. The pilot might be a Jap, but more likely he was an Aussie. The port hadn't been bombed yet from the air. The pilot must see that we were white men. Our very lack of activity topside would show we weren't enemies.

There was a tense minute or so, and then the plane made a wide sweep, dipped one wing in salute, and soared off into the distance. It had been a bad scare.

As we neared the port, we saw a familiar shape anchored in the bay—*"Ma" Holland*, our tender. We moored alongside. It was late afternoon early in 1942.

As we lay there, the U.S.S. *Tarpon* limped in. She looked as if she had weathered a terrific storm. And she had. We learned that she surfaced in a typhoon and nearly foundered. The *Tarpon* had no choice in the matter. Her batteries were down, and she had to surface. A giant wave came over after the hatch was opened, poured down the conning tower hatch, short-circuited radio and generators, and nearly flooded them out. The *Tarpon* couldn't dive after that; she was helpless to do anything but ride it out for three full days. For the first time in their lives nearly every man on the *Tarpon* was seasick.

The *Tarpon* was sent home later. She gave a good account of herself, though. She sank a pair of them on the way in.

But the *Tarpon* was soon forgotten. We wanted to get our cables off to our families, and when we finally did that, even though we couldn't say where we were, we were satisfied. Marjorie told me later that there was a knock on the door, a Western Union messenger delivered the telegram, and that it bore only my message and my signature. For all she knew, I might have sent it from Iceland or Timbuktu.

CHAPTER IV

Revenge for the Rock

WE FOUND the port a ghost town. When we got there most of the civilians had fled to the interior. The Japs were threatening the whole of Australia. They had bombed Rabaul in New Britain, they'd gained a foothold in New Guinea, and in the Solomons they'd bombed Tulagi and Kieta. The port was on the alert. The streets were deserted. Homes and stores were boarded up. It looked like a town in the tropics waiting for the hurricane to strike. The heat was terrific—the mercury simmered at no degrees.

Captain Warder said, "Go out and relax." He kept a skeleton crew aboard— only enough men to carry out essential work—overhauling engines, checking gear, refitting, adjusting. The rest of us broke out our whites, polished our shoes, and, spic and span, jumped into a liberty boat and chugged into dock, more than a mile away. The center of town was about a mile from the dock over a dry, dusty red-clay road. By the time we hiked there we were hot and perspiring and covered with dust. Our feet, accustomed so long to loose sandals, burned and ached. First we wanted ice-cold beer, and then we wanted new faces to see, new voices to hear. We wanted to hear a girl laugh and giggle, and watch the swing of her dress as she walked, and know how wonderful the world could be after days and nights in the cramped, prison-like confines of a submarine.

But we were out of luck. We couldn't get any beer; apparently the Aussies' thirst was for milkshakes, ice cream sodas, and similar sickening combinations. We explored for nearly an hour, growing more disgusted with every step. As for companionship, the only white woman we saw and spoke to was a hard-bitten, middle-aged waitress who had troubles of her own.

We took a vote and decided to return to the boat. At least, the *Wolf* had ice water and coffee. As we neared the ship again on the liberty boat, there was Lieutenant Deragon leaning in the shade of the conning tower, smoking a cigarette and watching a United States transport at anchor not far away.

We bobbed up and down alongside the rounded black sides of the *Wolf*. Deragon walked to the side and leaned over the heavy cable which serves as a rail. "What are you doing back here?" he demanded.

"Lieutenant," said Maley, in a hopeless voice, "there's nothing in port—no beer, no girls, no nothing."

"No beer?" Deragon said. He thought hard. "Well, I think we ought to be able to do something about that. You boys wait here," he said. He flipped his cigarette over the rail and hurried off.

We sat around smoking and comparing notes on things. They weren't complimentary. The sun came down, blazing hot. Not a breath of air anywhere. At the end of that dusty road, the port lay stewing in her own juice—a blistering hot town. Deragon showed up, perspiration rolling down his face.

"O.K.," he said. "I found a dozen cases of beer. They're on that transport. They're sending them over." He spoke so casually you might have thought he was giving us the time of day instead of a miracle. And while we sat there, our tongues hanging out, a launch came cutting through the water toward the *Seawolf*, carrying cases of cold beer under a tarpaulin. Beer—so far as the *Wolf* crew was concerned—meant baseball, and Gunner Bennett dashed down to the gun locker and came back with a seabag full of equipment—half a dozen bats, about a dozen balls and mitts. We found an empty lot, not far from the dock, unpacked our beer and equipment, and it was the engineers against the deck crew, the "Winton Wizards" vs. the "Deck Apes," with time out between innings to refresh ourselves. At the end of the fourth inning the score was 34 to 31, and no one knew who was leading.

"Aw, nuts," somebody said, and we called it a day. We finished the beer, packed up our softball equipment, and ambled happily back to the liberty boat and the *Wolf.*

We were in port several days. Quite a few uniforms paraded up and down the main avenue—Indian, Dutch, American, British. At night a gloom of its own settled upon the whitestone buildings and the hodgepodge of weather-beaten shacks. The Salvation Army had established one of their famous huts on the outskirts, a one-story green frame building. We munched free doughnuts, gulped what the Australians call coffee, and lounged in easy chairs. A middle-aged Australian couple were the staff.

But most of the time we had work to do aboard the *Wolf.*

Before supper of the last day, Sousa came bellowing through the ship. "All right, sailors, take it easy for a while and eat a good chow. Tonight we're really going to labor."

"What are you talking about?" someone asked him. "Work? Work on what?"

"Never mind the comment," said Sousa. "Do like I'm telling you."

That night two dim lights were rigged up on the conning tower, and about 8 p.m. a string of motor launches came out of the darkness. They were jammed with boxes of ammunition. We looked at them, swore, and set to work unloading them.

"What the hell," someone said bitterly, "are we a sub or a transport? Now they're making a cargo carrier out of us."

"Yeah," said Swede Enslin. "Put a smokestack and some lifeboats on us, and we'll go out disguised as a tramp steamer."

Jap ships were everywhere, waiting to be sunk, and here we were again, wasting our time acting like a freighter. The crew felt indignant. I think we began to see the light when Captain Warder ordered a number of torpedoes taken out of the *Wolf* and put on the *Holland* to make more room for ammunition. If the Skipper went so far as to take off our warheads—well, this job we were doing must be important. We felt better when the word came around that we were carrying this ammunition—anti-aircraft and machine-gun ammunition—to Corregidor, to the Rock. We were going to take this ammunition for our boys right through the Jap blockade, right through every ship and subchaser and destroyer the Japs could put there, and we'd take it to the boys on the Rock so they could hold Corregidor as long as human heart and muscle and skill could hold it. And for the record, too, we'd settle once and for all one of the oldest arguments in sub circles—just how valuable a submarine could be as a cargo carrier. If we got this cargo into the Rock, there'd be practically nothing the *Wolf* couldn't do except fly over it.

We packed ammunition until it almost oozed out. We thought the cases would never stop coming down. Ammunition piled higher and higher. It was in the forward torpedo room, the after-torpedo room. We stepped over it and we slept on it. The cases were above the level of my bunk, seven feet above the deck. That night I crawled over cases of shells to get to my bunk. Sleeping on that ammunition gave us a queer feeling. A heavy depth charge, with us packed in explosives like china in excelsior—"Well," said Maley, summing it up, "if they get us, they'll just blow us a little higher, that's all."

When we finally pulled away, the only torpedoes the *Wolf* had were those in her tubes, but she carried tons of ammunition.

We slid steadily through the waters north of Australia.

We traveled submerged in daylight and surfaced at night as usual. We were running at periscope depth, taking observations every few minutes, when Sousa's voice boomed over the intercom: "Call the Captain!"

Captain Warder went flying up into the conning tower. I heard Lieutenant Holden say: "Captain, I see something on the starboard bow. Can't make it out."

"Let's take a look at it, Dick," said Captain Warder. A thirty-second pause as he peered through the periscope. "She's pretty far off yet." Thoughtfully he added: "It could be a ship, all right. Let's continue as we are. Down periscope."

Three minutes later he upped the periscope again. He took his bearings, giving them to Lieutenant Holden: "Mark, three four six ..." Then, after a minute: "Mark three four seven ... That's pretty steady bearing. She's coming almost directly toward us, or she's going directly away from us." He waited, then: "Mark, three five two. That's a ship, all right. Coming this way, angle on the bow, five degrees starboard. It's a big one. Pretty far off yet, but looks like an aircraft carrier." Pause. "Battle stations!"

Again the battle alarm. The approach party took over the conning tower and began computing the approach course, the distance of the target, the speed and direction. Ten slow minutes went by. It was "Up periscope" again. "Mark, three five seven," began the Captain. "Range ... wait a minute! Wait ... a ... minute!"

Then, in a disgusted voice, "Secure battle stations." Pause. "Dick, come over here a minute and take a look at this ship you sighted."

Then Holden's voice, crestfallen: "Well, I'll be damned. A seagull floating on a log!"

The entire ship snickered. For days afterward, the crew greeted each other, "How we going to attack this here seagull? Shoot torpedoes at him or get up and fire a three-inch? Anybody got a slingshot?" And, "Baby, fresh meat—and we let him go!"

Then, hour after hour, no excitement. I caught up on my mending. I sewed up every bit of torn clothing I had. We gave Baby, the washing machine, a good workout. We resorted to all the old time-killing arguments. For three days I called upon heaven to witness that "Give me two spoonsful of sugar," was correct, and for three days Sully stamped through the *Seawolf* shaking the bulkheads, roaring that "Give me two spoonfuls" was correct. We held spelling bees as we lay in our bunks, resting our heels on the cases of ammunition.

"O.K., Eck, let's hear you spell *separate*," Lambertson, a husky fellow from Nebraska, his full beard making him look like a House of David baseball player, would sing out. Sometimes Sully broke the monotony by digging up one of his prized possessions, a dog-eared copy of an old *Consumers' Guide*. He swore by it. If *Consumers' Guide* failed to give a product a clean bill of health, Sully'd have none of it. We played blackjack, poker, and hearts in the mess hall, and we listened to Tokyo Rose and to 'Frisco. The news wasn't good. Tokyo Rose always told us we were being pushed back, and 'Frisco had a news commentator whose smooth voice got on our nerves. The only man on the boat who believed him was "Short Pants" Hershey. Hershey came from a farm in Wisconsin. He was thin-faced, slim, and wiry. He'd been wrestling champ of the Navy at 132 pounds, and he believed the best of everyone. Sitting back on a stool with his feet on a bulkhead pipe in the mess hall, he'd say, "You don't like the sound of his voice, that's all. That hasn't got anything to do with the truth of what he's saying. He's giving you the news."

Zerk would snap back, "I don't like the sound of that news. If what he says is true, why are we rushing this flea powder up to the Rock? Why isn't the fleet steaming out here and brushing the Nips off like he says they're about to do?"

"Well, Zerk, give them a little time," Hershey would say.

"They've got to get organized. That takes a lot of planning."

"Planning, hell!" retorted Zerk. "I'll tell you why—the Nips have so damned many ships out in this country that our fleet just can't stand up to them!"

"Hey, Zerk!" I interrupted. "What Navy you in, anyhow?"

That started him off. He pushed back from the table, slammed his fist down until the coffee cups jumped, and shouted: "Well, I'll be a son-of-a-bitch if that isn't the pay off! I was in this Navy when you all were just a glimmer in your old man's eye. I'm telling you what I think. I only hope there's enough land left the Nips haven't claimed yet so I can get a couple of beers."

He walked over to Hershey, who sat, mild and uninterested, and stuck his finger almost into his face:

"I'm not much of a flag-waver, squirt. I've been out in this country a hell of a lot longer than most of you, and I know those hissers. They're smart. They're the best little sneaks in the world. We'll be fighting these Japs a hell of a long time from now, and when it's over we'll know we've been in one hell of a fight."

John Street pushed in. "I got the book here," he said mildly. "Let's look at the figures. We've sunk ..."

"Oh, Jesus," someone groaned. "Street and his figures!"

"We've sunk a hell of a lot of Jap ships," Street said, unruffled, but Zerk wasn't listening.

"You know what the Japs sunk?" he demanded.

Sousa, who hadn't taken any part so far, leaned over. "Hey, Zerk," he said in that voice of his that sounded like a foghorn, "is it true you put in for a transfer to a Japanese sub?"

Zerk kicked his chair away. "Goddamn if I know why I waste my time talking to you dumb bastards," he exclaimed and stalked away.

The *Seawolf* moved steadily north. We were on a time schedule with our valuable cargo. We dared not waste too much time snooping around for trouble. But one night when the periscope was upped for a look, the sudden cry came, "Down periscope. Call the Captain!" Enemy ships had been sighted.

Captain Warder at the periscope described them. "One, two, three, four. It's a Jap task force: three or four big cruisers, a dozen destroyers, seven transports, a whole fleet of 'em! Here's a cruiser ... Seems to be head man here. He's using a searchlight. They're probably heading for a rendezvous ... Maybe I could get in and attack here. Must be another invasion force ... Well, now, what the hell am I supposed to do here? I'm carrying a whole load of stuff up to the Rock. My orders state that my prime mission is to deliver same. Here are some ships, and I've got only four fish forward and four fish aft, and that's all ..."

In the sound room Maley and I looked at each other. If we attacked, a hundred to one we'd be depth charged, and with these explosives ...

Captain Warder finally decided the all-important thing was to get the ammunition through. We moved on. But a few minutes later he came into the sound shack.

"Eck," he said, "here's the rough draft of an urgent dispatch. Send it as soon as we surface."

It was a message to the American Submarine High Command, revealing where we'd seen the Jap ships, their estimated course, their estimated speed. I sent it the moment we surfaced, and felt better thinking that we'd set up a welcome party for the Japs farther down the line.

We were gliding along on the surface that night when, about 2 a.m., off the port beam and not farther away than 1,000 yards, a huge dark shape loomed up

56

making terrific speed. In a minute or two the lookouts yelled, "It's a Jap destroyer!" She was probably late for the rendezvous to which we saw the others racing. It seemed impossible that she hadn't seen us. We were already starting a crash dive. In almost less time than it takes to tell, we were down to a safe distance under the water. Only seconds later the destroyer's propellers roared overhead, but apparently she had not seen us, because nothing happened. After we heard her screws die away, we eased up, looked around, saw the sea was clear, and surfaced and continued on our way. It was one of our narrowest escapes, and we got out of it probably because the destroyer was concentrating so intently upon reaching the rendezvous that she completely overlooked us.

I've often thought what would have happened had that destroyer suddenly veered hard left and headed for us. It would have been touch and go. With the ammunition aboard, that might have been *the* attack and the *Seawolf*'s end.

Hour by hour we came nearer beleaguered Corregidor. The Jap blockade was heavier than ever. We left the Sulu Sea, and entered the South China Sea and set our course directly for the Rock. This time the Japs were everywhere. Their planes swarmed over the place. The Skipper saw them, and smiled grimly, and lowered his periscope, and the *Wolf* moved on, hour after hour, nursing her tons of hot lead waiting to be hurled against the Jap invaders.

We made it into Corregidor without being detected. During the night we were again escorted in by a PT boat. Again we slowly passed through the heavy mine field. Our lines were no sooner fast to the dock than we were sweating away unloading our ammunition. It was impossible to unload so enormous a cargo in one night. We dared not remain tied to the dock during daylight. Before dawn we eased out into deep water, submerged, and lay on the bottom until nightfall. Dusk came, then darkness. We surfaced. We stole back into the dock, and finished unloading. Then, at last, some of us had an opportunity to go ashore and see what was going on.

In the midst of a brilliant starlit night, I walked over the gangplank and stepped upon the same wooden dock I had been upon four weeks before. Our men now were making the bravest kind of a stand that a man can make: they were fighting off an enemy who grew stronger every hour. As I breathed slowly, grateful for the fresh air, I heard the distant thunder of the Jap guns on Bataan, twenty miles away. There was activity all around me, but it was weirdly silent. Soldiers hurried by, struggling with the ammunition we'd piled on the dock. Men were standing about in small groups. They watched and said nothing. As I stood there, the wind veered and the most nauseating stench I ever smelled hit me. I needed a cigarette bad. I dug into my pocket for one and was about to strike a match when a voice sounded at my elbow.

"I wouldn't light that if I were you, buddy," it said.

I turned. It was a soldier. The moonlight glinted off the Tommy gun he had slung over his shoulder. "No lights allowed anywhere," he said. "We're under blackout conditions." I threw my cigarette away. His face was hardly visible, but he looked young. "They pushing you around much up here?" I asked. His reply was typical of the 31st Infantry, and I think it represented what was in the minds of the men on Corregidor then. Yes, things were tough, but they were holding out. After all, this was the end of January; they did not capitulate until May. As for Jap successes—"Naw," he said, with contempt. "We're averaging better than fifty to one against those little bastards. Sure, we're having trouble, but the Japs aren't the cause of it."

Food bothered them, he said. Rice, and more rice. They were sick of it. They were eating only twice a day now, and mostly rice. Typhoid was breaking out. About the only exercise they got was at noon when the Jap planes came over and the men ran for shelter. The Nip bombers, he said, came over every day. "You can set your watch by them. But we're knocking 'em out of the sky like clay pigeons. The other day one of our three-inch anti-aircraft set a world record. Knocked down eight planes in one day. We figure more than 80 percent of their bombs fall into the water."

At that moment the wind veered again.

"What is that?" I demanded. "Christ, what is that smell?"

"Yeah," said the soldier, "I know. It's Japs. Those are dead Japs you're smelling. We got thousands of them laying around these hills. They're not burying them and—well, when the wind's right ..."

That was it. The stench of death hung sickeningly over Corregidor. In these waters about us, in these hills vaguely etched against the horizon, lay bloated, mutilated bodies. During the day that fierce equatorial sun beat down on them, and at night the smell of death was overpowering. But the soldier was talking again. How long were we staying? I didn't know, I said. All I knew was, they needed ammunition and we brought it to them.

Did I think help was on the way?

I said I thought the fleet should be coming along pretty soon.

"I wasn't wondering so much about the big fleet," he said. "But we sure could use some planes. Those damn Japs cavort around up there, and our pea-slingers can't always reach that high. We knocked down a few foolish ones, but that did the trick. Now they just go a little higher."

The next night I was able to go into Corregidor itself. I wanted to see what it was like, and I wanted to pick up a few radio parts if they could spare them. In the darkness, wearing sandals and shorts and shirt, a heavy growth of beard on my face, I walked up the dusty road and got my first glimpse of the island fortress, 600 feet high, that splits the Bay of Manila, and was then known as the biggest and most impregnable fort in the world. None of its defenses could be seen from the sea or sky. The gun emplacements were beautifully hidden by trees planted to hide them. It was magnificent.

As I looked at the Rock, there in the gloom, I thought, *Corregidor may fall, but the Japs will pay for it.*

Finally I came to the mouth of a tunnel at the base of a cliff. I was amazed at the brilliance inside. It was as bright as day, and I had to shield my eyes at first against the hard white light. I saw men sleeping everywhere. They lay rolled up in blankets; dozed sitting on chairs and cases of ammunition. Here two men were lining a number of hospital cots against a wall. A little farther on, a group of soldiers were standing about a small cigar stand, chatting and exchanging gossip as men do around cigar stands anywhere in the world. Half a dozen soldiers hurried by me, carrying large galvanized cans. They stared at me. I guess I looked like a hermit come out of the hills.

"What's in that can?" I asked.

"Chlorinated drinking water," one soldier said.

"Wait a minute," I called. "What tunnel is this?"

He paused for a minute. "Malinta tunnel," he said. "You looking for anything in particular?"

I told him I was looking for Communications.

"Straight ahead," he said. "Keep going."

I kept going. I passed massive steel doors on either side of the tunnel leading to smaller tunnels, and finally came to one door behind which I was told I'd find Communications. I put my hand on the knob.

A navy ensign appeared from nowhere. "Just a minute, please," he said crisply. "Where are you going?"

I identified myself and told him.

"I'm sorry," he said. "I don't think we can permit you to go in there now. They're just too damn busy, and you wouldn't have a very good chance of finding what you want anyway."

I decided the best thing for me to do was get out of the way.

My place was on the *Seawolf*. I returned the way I came. Walking back to the dock, I could see searchlights playing up and down the shoreline of Mariveles, the naval base about a mile to the north, hunting the Japs along the mainland. Now and then, the *rat-a-tat-tat* of machine-gun fire came to my ears, and I could hear the dull thud of artillery fire from Bataan. Every few minutes brilliant white flares split the darkness off toward Mariveles. Searchlights continued to move their fingers across the sky.

I went aboard the *Seawolf* and down where I belonged—in the sound room. That was the last picture I had of Corregidor.

CHAPTER V

Rescue of the Bamboo Fleet

IT WAS later that we surfaced and stole in to the dock again. We had not been there ten minutes when a military truck rumbled down to the dock, and out of it came more than a score of the most disreputable human beings in Army uniform I had seen. They looked as if they might have stepped by magic right off New York's Bowery. They were gaunt, and their fatigue uniforms were dirty and tattered. I caught one glimpse of them and then was called below. Our visitors came abroad. I wondered who they were.

Then a message came down: "All passengers on deck."

Passengers? I thought. What were we up to now? After acting as a transport all over the Far East, were they going to turn us into a ferry? Maley solved it for me when I took up my post next to him.

"We got passengers aboard," I said. "Now all I'm asking is that they keep out of my way and out of this shack."

"Aw, take it easy, Eck," Maley said. "They're fliers. They've been shot down, and a lot of them are pretty goddamn heroes, too." He was topside when they all came on, twenty-six of them, he said, and he heard an Army officer give them a little pep talk. It ran something like this, said Maley:

"Men, we're fortunate to leave the Rock on this submarine. We're more than fortunate because this ship has a good crew and it is clean. I want everyone here to remember that he is a passenger, and that the crew has work to do. Stay out of their way. They aren't too eager for this hauling duty, anyway. There will be plenty of food, but frankly, I don't know what you're going to do about sleep. There may be an empty bunk once in a while. If you're sure that some crew member isn't due to use it, then you can lie down. Remember that we're depending upon these people to get us where we're going. We're leaving in a few minutes now; so go below, get in a corner, and be quiet."

I had to admit they were quiet, too, and that they made the best of things. There was scarcely any room on the *Wolf* for them.

We shoved off that night, but before we left, we loaded many more boxes of valuable material, and this took every cubic foot of space left. At midnight we started out of the harbor to run the Jap blockade once more. If space was at a premium on our trip in, now there wasn't room to move anywhere.

Finally an arrangement of hot bunks was worked out. The *Wolf's* crew and the aviators slept in relays, and during the eight-day trip every bunk on the boat had someone sleeping in it every hour of the day. Even that was not sufficient;

and going through the boat, now and then you'd see an aviator sleeping on his feet—leaning against a bulkhead catching forty winks. Some fell asleep while they were eating.

The Japs were looking high and low for us as we sneaked out of Manila Harbor. Two or three times in the darkness it seemed as though their planes might have discovered us, but the *Wolf* outsmarted them, and by dawn we were far enough out to be comparatively safe.

I had my hands full on sound as we went through the blockade, and had little chance to stroll around and get a good glance at our passengers. But at 8 a.m., after my morning watch, I went forward to the forward torpedo room and saw two of them near my bunk. They were just youngsters, and they looked worn out. They were discarding some of their personal gear—gas masks, knives, and belts—and I couldn't help overhearing their conversation.

"D'you know," one of them, a young kid with a scar on his face, was saying, "you can get hot coffee anytime you want on this ship? They got sandwiches, fruit—why, it's like being on a goddamn luxury liner."

I began to cool down. Hot coffee ... sandwiches ... why, we were always griping because the meat was too rare or too well done.

The other aviator spoke up. "All I got to say is I'm sure glad to get on. As far as I'm concerned, I'll stand right here until we hit port and won't say a damned thing."

My conversation with the sentry on the dock came back to me. These men must have gone through hell like all the rest of the boys on the Rock.

"If I just took my cleaning gear and stowed it here, do you think anybody'd get sore?" the fellow with the scar said.

His gear was a canvas dressing kit with toothbrush, tooth paste, soap, and comb. Rolled up, it was no larger than a man's fist. I'd heard enough. All my antagonism vanished.

I stepped up. "Bud, you're sharing my cleaning-gear locker," I said. "I haven't got much in there, and there's plenty of room."

I don't think he could have been twenty-two. He was so grateful, I felt like a skunk. As the days went on and I learned his story, I knew that we should have been damn proud to carry such passengers. He had been shot down twice by Jap Zeros. He had been flying a PBY—the old Navy flying boat, which could do only about 140 knots with everything bent on it.

The others had been through the mill, too. One had been shot down three times. Some had been forced to make their way for miles through semi-jungles and swamps before they reached the safety of the American lines. The *Seawolf*'s crew stopped griping about ferrying passengers and we filled those boys full of good submarine food, warmed them up with good hot coffee, and couldn't do too much for them. They were amazed at the good food, the variety of it—steak, ham, lamb and pork chops, the pies and pastries we served. They grinned when they came in for breakfast and saw Doc Loaiza going through his daily routine of placing two vitamin pills at each plate.

We learned of the problems they faced fighting the Japs. Principally, they needed faster planes. "Those Zeros against what we had made it just like the old turtle and hare story," we were told. "Those Jap ships are going to be mighty tough to get around, even with our new pursuits, because they're so fast and maneuverable." The youngster who was sharing my locker had been sent up "without definite orders," he said. "Everybody could see the finale was coming, so we just went up with the idea of taking a smack at them whenever we spotted anything. I got in several good smacks, but I got smacked in return—twice by Zeros and once by the heaviest curtain of flak I've ever seen. I was lucky. I managed to bail out every time. Some of the boys didn't. I know I wouldn't have given much for my chances going down in a 'chute. The Japs butcher a man in the silk just like they do everything else. But I managed to get back every time, and now I guess the big boys have decided I've had enough." He grinned. "They tell me I'm a little punchy. Maybe so. I'm inclined to believe them myself. All I want now is a good plane and a good crew, and then let me at 'em!"

The crew adopted the men. We showed them how we made our leisure time go by in Kelly's Pool Room—cribbage, hearts, dice, acey-deucy. We let them wash their clothes in Baby, and they got a kick out of watching us in the evening, sitting on our bunks and darning socks or sewing buttons.

We loosened up and had fun with them. I sent some of them here and there for oxygen pumps and nitrogen needles and other tools that didn't exist. One fellow, a boy from New York City, wandered into the sound shack.

"Come in," I said. "Make yourself at home. I've got something to show you."

"Thanks," he said, "I was kind of looking for a place to park in."

"Well, as long as you're here, I might as well explain some of these gadgets to you," I told him. "See that thing right over your head?" It was the direction finder loop antenna. "That's what we call an oxometer."

"Never heard of it," he said. "What did you say it was?"

"Oxometer." I spelled it out to him. "O-x-o-m-e-t-e-r. It's a pretty complicated piece of gear, but it's damned important, especially now that we have you people aboard."

He looked surprised. "Is that so? Say, let me know about it, will you? Maybe I'd be able to give you a hand one of these days."

"Oh," I said, "the operation is quite simple. You merely stand over here and vary this control"—I pointed to the handle on the direction finder loop— "and watch that meter over there." This was the sensitivity meter on the direction-finder receiver.

"And what does that do?"

"I'm telling you," I said. "When that needle passes this point, that's the danger signal. Then you bend down and roll up your trousers right to the knee."

His mouth almost fell open. "My God, you mean water is coming in?"

"No," I said. "Not water. This oxometer measures the flow of bull going fore and aft, and we have to prepare to walk through it. It's been near the danger point ever since you fellows came aboard."

"Why, you red-headed bastard!" he began, and then broke down laughing.

Now and then in the course of a routine test, we'd let a little air hiss out of a valve, and some wisecracker would whisper, loud enough for our passengers to hear, "Jeez, the Skipper's taking her down to 1,000 feet." The faces of the aviators would be a sight.

The thought of going down 1,000 feet under the water didn't make them any too happy. Of course, no submarine can go that deep. This kind of tomfoolery went on all the way south. As we plowed on, we came into warmer waters. The water temperature ranged from the high 80's into the 90's, and our aviators never seemed to get over the fact that the *Wolf* was air-conditioned and that we could be so comfortable in those hot waters.

At night, when we surfaced, we caught up with the progress of the war. American and Dutch destroyers and planes had gone into the Macassar Straits and practically wiped out a Jap convoy.

That was our first knowledge of the great Macassar Straits battle, in which more than 50 Jap transports were sunk and perhaps as many as 25,000 Jap soldiers lost. This mass sinking was the best news we had heard for a long time. We knew it was all a surface affair and we were amazed that our old destroyers could do so well. About the fifth night out, with sea and sky black as pitch, we thought we might get a little action of our own. Over on our starboard bow a shape gloomed up just on the edge of visibility. A Jap submarine running awash? The battle alarm jangled through the boat. Our aviators squeezed into corners, fascinated, as the *Wolf*'s men clicked into position. We started to ease up for a shot. Then from the conning tower came a disgusted exclamation: "Oh, nuts! It's a log with a branch on it!"

Two nights later the lookout saw what appeared to be a ship with mast and smokestack. We made a crash dive and deployed for a target very cautiously. I was at sound and absolutely miserable. I could hear nothing; no screws, no pings, nothing—only the ceaseless crackle of the water. Each time the Skipper asked, "Do you have anything?" I had to report, "Nothing on sound, sir."

"Up periscope," came from the Captain. Then—"Damn it!"—sharp and clear. "It's a little island."

If there are sea gremlins, they were certainly having a time with us.

We surfaced and continued on our course. We entered Macassar Straits, and finally we reached the great naval base of Surabaya, Java.

For weeks the Japs had been aiming for this chief base of operations for the United Nations in the Dutch East Indies, and when we arrived, Surabaya had already been dive-bombed three times in as many days.

We drew up to dock midafternoon. The sun shone like a brass plate. We had been going steadily since December 8—almost two months—and for most of that time most of us never saw daylight.

We tied up at Holland Pier. Less than 100 yards away we saw the evidence of Jap bombing—huge ten-foot craters in the road-way, where at least a dozen 500-pounders had landed. They struck several barracks—gray wood frame structures—and the roofs were smashed and splintered. Elsewhere fire-blackened charred walls pointed to the Japs' fury.

Our twenty-six aviators looked much better when they stepped out on dock than when they came aboard. They were surprised to find themselves in Surabaya; they thought they were being taken to Australia. We shook hands all around. We really enjoyed having them aboard. For some reason the average submarine man and the average aviator aren't too friendly. When a submarine begins a mission, it has no friends. Everyone must be considered an enemy, for a submarine flies no flags and from the distance all subs look alike—particularly to aviators. We were always wary of aircraft. Medal-hungry fliers will bomb anything resembling a submarine. Only the airplane could see us below the surface. It was our natural enemy. It was as though a natural antagonism exists between these two services whose medium is so different—one air, the other water.

When we arrived in Surabaya, it was under almost its first concerted bombing of the war. The very first raid had come only four days ago, when nearly eighty Jap bombers, with a tremendous fighter escort, raided the harbor, and aimed many of their bombs on the large hotels in town, thinking the Dutch and U.S. High Command was there.

We waited until a tall, gangling Navy lieutenant came aboard, a .45 at his hip, and a satchel in his hand. He was the paymaster, and he was escorted by two sailors both sporting .45's. He gave us a week's pay in Dutch guilders. Then there was more excitement. Gus Wright came into the mess hall with a five-gallon can.

"Milk," someone shouted, and we went for it.

Gus pulled off the cover, stuck a dipper in it, and we gathered around and gulped down fresh milk until we were bloated.

Then we went ashore. The town was so busy we could hardly believe our eyes. We hadn't seen anything like it for a long time. But, after all, this was the third greatest naval base in the East, second only to Singapore and Hong Kong. A jetty more than a half-mile long lay along the harbor's entrance, and here thousands of barrels of oil were daily piped into tankers for the vessels of the Allied nations. One glance, and I knew the Japs weren't having much trouble finding this base from the air. Two rivers outlined it clearly.

In the town, trolleys jammed with people—whites, blacks, turban-crowned Orientals, and slim, brown-skinned Javanese—rattled through the busy streets. Most of the large buildings were painted a sickly green—part of a camouflage plan. The streets were colorful. Brilliant-saronged natives brushed elbows with army and navy men dressed in almost every uniform of the Allied nations. Rawboned Australians, looking more like Texans than Texans themselves, strode along wearing their traditional up-swept hats. The city was dotted with large onion-shaped air-raid shelters, about thirty feet high, camouflaged green to blend in with Surabaya's vegetation. Dutch soldiers walked through the streets with huge eighteen-inch Luger pistols in their holsters.

The crew of the *Wolf* wandered about town, gorging themselves on fresh fruit piled up in the open markets, visiting the bars with their half-size swinging doors, and catching up on air and light and sunshine.

Our second day in town Captain John Wilkes, U.S. Submarine Squadron Commander, told Captain Warder that a rest camp had been established at Malang, a tiny town high in the mountains about fifty miles south of Surabaya. The crew was divided into two sections, one to stay and repair the ship, the other to go to Malang for three days; then the crew sections alternated, and the second group was to have its three days' rest. We were to be guests of the local Dutch naval garrison.

I was in the first group. We started for the railway station in town the morning of our third day and got there just as the air-raid sirens began to wail. We were all in whites and conspicuous from the air. We'd been told the Japs kept an eye out for white uniforms. The Javanese natives milled about, panic-stricken; we tried to reassure them by moving casually through the crowd. Lieutenant Holden suggested that we better get out of the station. One of the first objectives of bombers is a railway station. We climbed a twenty-foot embankment and found ourselves in a rice field, with about six inches of water in it. Water or no water, we crouched in the field and waited.

The planes came over a minute later, twenty-seven in formations of V's, flying high and straight. They paid no attention to the railway station, however; they continued toward the water front and dropped their bombs there. We heard the explosions. Then, a minute later, they were roaring back—only one plane missing. Surabaya's aircraft defenses were pretty bad then.

We enjoyed ourselves at Malang. We met a radio operator there from a Dutch submarine, who was in a pitiful state. He was one of two survivors; his boat had been sunk by Jap depth charges near Java, in very shallow water, and it sank with an angle at the bow. The two escaped through torpedo tubes. He was still shaky, and as he talked about it a muscle in his jaw pulsed and twitched. He had lost all his teeth during the ordeal. And he'd come to Malang to get himself a brand-new set of store teeth.

Jap bombing planes came over Malang daily, but they didn't bother with the little resort. They were hunting a large bomber airfield a couple of miles away, but so cleverly camouflaged by the Dutch that the Japs never located it—at least, not while we were there. We'd watch our own B-17's take off each morning, and then a few hours later the Japs would sail by, probably cursing as they searched in vain for the field.

We were called back to the *Wolf* at the end of our third day. In Surabaya we learned the *Wolf* had been forced to go through her regular hide-and-seek routine. The air-raids never let up; the Japs were methodical, roaring over the water front between 9 and 10 a.m. The *Wolf* would nose out into the bay before 9 a.m., submerge, and cruise about or lie on the bottom. At dusk she returned to the dock again.

We wondered why new orders hadn't arrived. We were ready to register a loud protest if they meant ferry duty again. But at last Captain Warder came briskly aboard after a conference, and his first order was to take on a full allowance of warhead torpedoes.

That meant action. Our freighting days were over. And we got action—far more than we ever bargained for.

CHAPTER VI

Fire One! . . . Fire Two!

"TAKE IN all lines." Captain Warder's voice rang out in the darkness. The great Dutch port of Surabaya lay about us in a half-circle, blacked out against the enemy.

"All back one-third!"

The U.S.S. *Seawolf* trembled as she backed into the harbor.

We turned around until we were headed due north. Heavy with fuel and food and torpedoes, we began snaking our way through the mine-filled waters on our fifth mission of the war, once again charged with unrestricted submarine warfare—to sink and destroy enemy shipping wherever encountered. It was still early in 1942; the Japanese juggernaut, triumphantly crushing all resistance, was roaring southward with growing fury; and the *Seawolf*, done at last with assignments as transport and ferry, was on her way to glory. We had aboard a Dutch pilot who knew every inch of these waters, the position of every mine. By his side on the bridge stood Captain Warder, and together they peered through the darkness as we moved forward, gliding past the dark shapes of wharves and jetties with their cranes grotesque against the purple sky. Above the steady purring of the *Wolf*'s Diesels came the sharp *chug! chug!* of a motor. The *Wolf* came to a halt, riding in a mirror-smooth sea; a flurry of conversation on the bridge, and the pilot, with a wave of his hand, climbed over. The *Wolf* moved on, alone.

Our bow was pointed for Macassar Straits, between Borneo and the Celebes. The Dutch were fighting a desperate delaying action, aided by Flying Fortresses operating from secret bases in Java, against the Japs who had to cross Macassar Straits to get to the rich oil wells of Borneo. At midnight of the second day I received a short coded dispatch which was rushed to the Skipper. A few minutes later the *Wolf* veered sharply to the right, reversed her course, and, working up to full power, raced back the way she came. The news spread swiftly. We were going to Lombok Straits, a narrow passage between Lombok and the island of Bali, 120 miles southeast of Surabaya. The Japs' southward push to gain that great semicircular chain of islands, Java, Bali, Lombok, Flores, and Timor, which alone stood between the Japs and Australia, had gained such momentum that they had already overrun the Celebes Sea area, our original destination. Now our job was to get to the Lombok Straits and impede that southward avalanche. At any other time we might have been excited about skirting the coast of romantic Bali, but now the *Wolf*'s crew was all business. The Japs were cleaning up; no one could stop them. How swiftly they were coming down we learned with shocking suddenness that night when radio frequency told us Singapore had fallen. The Japs had taken it the very day we left Surabaya. There were grim faces aboard the *Wolf*. Singapore gone? That had been a symbol of might and resistance before any of us had been born. The picture of Japanese strategy—hedgehopping island by island—became clearer, and so did the part we were to play. The Japs wanted Java; their aim was to smash the Dutch defenses protecting Bali which would be one of their stepping-stones to Surabaya. From Sumatra they would cross the Sunda Straits eastward; from Bali they would cross westward, and from Borneo and the Celebes southward; and with an endless supply of men and matériel, they would launch a triumphant blow against Java, heart of the barrier. Once Java was theirs, Surabaya with its invaluable harbor, its magnificent naval installations, its inexhaustible riches, would be in their hands.

Captain Warder sent the *Wolf* plunging forward with every ounce of power we could muster. Twenty-four hours later found us at the entrance of the Lombok Straits, struggling in some of the most dangerous and unpredictable water currents in the world. We dove at daylight, and through the long hours the *Wolf* fought to maintain her course submerged. Depth control and navigation were extremely difficult. Every inch was a battle. The waters were shallow, and vicious cross currents made them treacherous. Sometimes we moved for six hours in one direction, only to learn that we had not gained a foot, actually, but had even been forced backward. The crew was tense. No matter how dangerous surface waters may be, there are always guides—sun, stars, shore points—by which you can set your course. But under the sea everything must depend upon the navigator and his estimate of the ship's position, and upon what sound tells him: how far, how fast, and in what direction the underwater currents may be taking the ship off her course.

As we laboriously maneuvered with Bali on our left and Lombok on our right, we heard more news. None of it was good.

Now the Japs were bringing their offensive to pinpoint focus. They were concentrating a tremendous force on one assault, to take the Bali airfield. They might even attempt a landing on Bali, under our nose. Captain Warder picked the most logical place for the Nips to attempt such a landing, and we kept that under close observation. A British submarine, we learned, was posted at the northern entrance of the straits. One of our older S submarines was assigned to the central area; and we were given the southern entrance. We patrolled carefully, day and night, awaiting the Japs. Then came a message from the High Command: urgent orders must pull the S boat elsewhere and we'd have to take over her area. Now our job was doubled. We lengthened our patrol. During the day the *Wolf* was alert within the straits, covering every point she could; at dusk she stole out through the southern entrance, surfaced, charged batteries, and ran the patrol back and forth in front of the entrance.

On the seventh night came another urgent message: *the Jap force had been sighted.* An armada of Jap men-of-war and transports was racing full speed for the Lombok Straits. The *Seawolf* was ordered to meet it head on. We halted our battery charge and at terrific speed knifed our way on the surface northward for the straits, plunged into them, and did not ease our Diesels until the dull mass of Nusa Besar, a small island in the middle of the channel, came into sight. We waited, watched, waited ...

"Something one point on the starboard bow, sir!" It was the bow lookout. The time was 2 a.m.

"Clear the bridge! Stand by to dive!"

Wang! went the klaxon horn signal. Men tumbled down the ladder, the hatch was swiggled tight, we crash dived and leveled off.

Now, on sound, I heard pinging all around. We'd gotten into a hornet's nest, all right. We didn't realize it then, but we had penetrated through the outer screen of Japanese destroyers—their first defense, specifically set up to intercept any enemy force—and were in the middle of the Jap task force.

Captain Warder upped his periscope carefully. "It's pitch black up here," he said. "I can't see a damn thing ... not a damn thing."

But in the sound shack, phones pressed against my ears, I heard the chorus of beating screws. Maley, who'd been dozing just before the diving alarm sounded, joined me. His long nose seemed even longer.

"Jesus," he said soberly, "I hear we're really in it."

"You're not kidding," I said. "We've got a whole nest of them up there."

He pulled a cigarette out of his shirt pocket and lit it. "I understand from the talk that we're heading right in," he said, staring at the red tip of his cigarette. "The old man's waiting until it comes light so he can see what he's doing. He's not interested in these destroyers, anyway. He wants the troop ships."

Overhead the Jap screws churned the sea. Their sound came down through the water and penetrated the ship's hull. Everyone heard it.

Maley inhaled deeply. The subdued light of the radio shack etched the hollows under his cheekbones. "It's going to be a long day," he said.

I said, "Yes, it looks like we're going to have quite a time."

Maley puffed again, suddenly ground out his cigarette, stood up impatiently, pulled at his ear, and wanted to know if I didn't want coffee. "I'll take over for a while," he said.

I looked at my watch: 5 a.m. I still had three hours to go. I recognized Paul's symptoms. He wanted to sit down and hear for himself. He wanted to size things up himself.

"Okay," I said. I gave him the phones and ambled aft into the mess hall. Half a dozen men were there, sipping coffee and complaining about it. The coffee was the first made from a batch of Javanese coffee we'd taken on at Surabaya, and though we knew it was supposed to be the best coffee in the world, we didn't like it. We thought it reeked.

"What we got up there?" someone asked. "Does it look like we're going to get it, Eck?"

I shrugged my shoulders. No use kidding ourselves. "The way I get it," I said, "we're in a whole damn swarm of ships. We got four or five Nip destroyers rushing around up there."

I was certain that eight or ten more were patrolling the entrance of the straits. We were in here tight, all right. I took my coffee back into the sound shack.

Maley gave me the phones with a tired smile. "They don't sound like they'd want to play games up there," he said. Then he went off to finish sleeping. At dawn the Skipper brought us up to periscope depth. He scanned the sea. "Well, I'll be damned," he said. "What do you think of that? Down periscope." Then, to Ensign Mercer: "Jim, there's nothing up there now. Nothing at all. Let me see those charts." It was evident that the destroyers had spread out and were running an entrance patrol, completely unaware that we were already inside. I was right. We were locked in the straits.

Silence for a moment, then Captain Warder's voice again: "We dove at this point, didn't we? We've been making one-third. That means we should be in here somewhere."

"That's right, sir," came Mercer's voice.

"Up periscope," said the Captain. "Dammit ... dammit if I don't think I'm lost. I can't spot Nusa Besar. I see some land over there, but I don't know where it is on the chart. Do you suppose this current has thrown us off again? ... *Hmmmmm* ... Well, we're bound to run into them if we continue up the straits. We certainly can't miss them. There's too many."

We moved on slowly, hour after hour. We were moving north in the straits, but we did not know our exact position. The Skipper took frequent periscope observations.

"Aha," he said, some minutes later. "I see the masts of several big ships. They're close to the beach. They're probably where we thought they were, over near that Bali airfield. They look as if they're at anchor. Now, Jim ... if that's the airfield, mark my bearing." He estimated the distance. "Range, 16,000 yards." Then: "Now we ought to get an idea where we are. Don't sound battle stations yet. I want to get this navigational problem fixed up before I attack. I've got to make sure of what I'm getting into here, and I've got to find a way out."

Minutes passed. The Skipper and Mercer were working at the plotting table. This was a damn important operation for the *Wolf*. If we could stop the Japs from landing on Bali, we could throw them off their timetable and delay their entire East Indies invasion. At this very moment the United Nations were pouring troops and munitions into the vital ports of Moresby and Darwin, building them up as supply bases. Every hour counted.

"All right!" Captain Warder sounded satisfied. "We'll get on the course to close with them. Tell the crew to stand easy. It'll be quite a while yet before we get in to where I'm going to fire."

We maneuvered slowly. We knew we were in treacherous waters and going into still more dangerous ones. Over my phones I heard the roar of shallow water eddying and swirling around the high coral shoals. The *Wolf* was weaving her way with infinite care through a subterranean maze of jagged, razor-sharp reefs, any one of which could rip her hull from stern to stern. The slightest error in navigation would be fatal for all of us. My watch showed a few minutes after 7 a.m. Gus Wright, battle telephones on his ears, was in the after-battery compartment, ready to pass on all orders from the conning tower. We were ready to leap into action. We glided forward smoothly. Suddenly the *Wolf* lurched. The lights flickered. I was thrown off my stool. There was a grinding, grating noise.

"We're aground!" someone shouted.

It echoed thinly through the ship.

Captain Warder's voice said: "All back emergency!"

The *Wolf* shuddered. We heard the grating noise again forward on the keel. Suddenly we were free. Down below we began breathing again.

"Well, Jim," said Captain Warder conversationally, "I guess we just won't go in that way. We'll have to find some other way in here."

We reversed our course. We inched backward. Suddenly, another lurch, a jar, and the *Wolf* was stuck again, this time at periscope depth. Ten full minutes the Skipper made use of all the tactics he knew for such an emergency. No one did much talking. We were in a hell of a spot. We were trapped, we were lost, and above us prowled Jap warships loaded with depth charges.

Captain Warder, at the control-room periscope, scanned the sea. The sun was shining, the day was bright. He could see the ships he wanted to attack, and he couldn't get at them. "I can't keep this up," he said. "I'll hurt her. She's going to get damaged. There are ships in there, and I've got to get them." He stepped back from the periscope. "Surface!" he snapped, and shinnied up the control-room ladder like a monkey.

Sitting in the sound shack, I felt my stomach turn over. I went ice cold. For the first time in my life I think I knew absolute, craven fear. Here it was bright daylight, and Captain Warder was bringing us up in the middle of a Jap task force that could blow us to bits with a single salvo.

The *Wolf* broke water. The hatch sprang open. The Captain raced to the bridge. I waited instinctively for the first shells to scream over.

Captain Warder's voice came down evenly: "Put two main engines on propulsion. Put two on quick battery charge." Then: "Send raincoats to the bridge."

Nothing made sense any more, and then all at once it did. As we surfaced, a tropical squall had struck us, as though in the *Wolf*'s extremity someone had cast a huge gray blanket over us, shielding us from the Japs. "An act of God," Captain Warder called it later. Dangerous as the surfacing appeared to us below, the Skipper was correct in his analysis of what had to be done. If we continued underwater, we might be caught on the coral reefs. Far better to risk getting out of these dangerous waters, with the chance of fighting it out on the surface, than to be set up like a sitting duck on a rock for the Japs.

We ran toward deeper water on the two engines, full speed, for about half an hour, and then we dove. It was our eleventh night out of Surabaya. As soon as we leveled off, I began searching for ships. Something was wrong. The familiar background of water noises was missing. The number two projector was dead. It must have snapped off the end of the second sound shaft when we ran aground. Now the *Wolf* was crippled in sound, badly crippled. There was nothing we could do to fix it. Now sound had only one projector with which to search and find the enemy, look out for other ships, and trace the trail of our torpedoes. I reported it to the Captain.

"Carry on the best you can, Eckberg," he said.

We moved in toward the beach. It was now 11 a.m. Captain Warder upped periscope. He saw three big transports jammed with Jap troops. He kept up a running report: "A destroyer over there ... That bastard is firing ... He's firing his main batteries. There they go—I can see the burst and flame and smoke .... Is he firing at me? He's firing in this direction, all right .... Hell, he can't see this periscope! ... Ohhhh. They're firing their anti-aircraft! There's something up there .... Well, that's fine!" He chuckled. "That takes the pressure right off us. Now we can really sneak in." Pause. "There's some Jap Zeros there, too, dammit."

We closed with the transports. We reached a point where the water was so shallow we could go no farther at periscope depth. Captain Warder ordered the *Wolf* swung about so that he could fire from the stern tubes and be headed out at the same time for a swift escape.

"Stand by!" came from the conning tower. Captain Warder coached Rudy at the helm. "Right a little ... Left a little ... Steady ... steady ... steady ... steady ..." This was a long-range shot. It had to be right. "Fire six!" A pause. "Fire seven!" A pause. "Fire eight!"

I picked up the torpedoes as they went.

"They're running hot, Captain," I reported. "I can hear them—"

"Yes, they're running straight, too, Eckberg," came Captain Warder's soft voice. "I'm watching them."

A minute later: "Oh, hell! Down periscope. *Rig for depth-charge attack!*"

This was the first time the Skipper had uttered those words.

My first reaction was simple curiosity. My pulses were beating at my temples, but through my mind ran the thought, *Here they come. I'm really going to get it this time. I wonder how I'm going to act. Am I going to be the screaming, raving type? Or am I going to be just another guy getting depth-charged? Was I—*

Captain Warder, slow and deliberate, broke in: "Now, Eckberg, here comes a destroyer. We are going to get hell. I want you to pick up those propellers, and I want you to give me bearings. Give me all the information you can in regard to this ship."

Under his words I heard three distant muffled explosions. Our fish had hit home. I answered him, surprised at my calm voice: "I sure will, Captain. I've got him now. I've got his screws. They're bearing one six zero, they're fast, and they're getting louder." The *whish-sh ... whish-sh ... whish-sh* of the destroyers' screws was clear in my phones.

"Good!" said the Captain.

"He's coming portside, Captain, he's coming fast."

"Very well, Eckberg. Keep talking."

"Aye, aye, sir."

Now every moving thing in the *Wolf*—every bit of machinery, every source of sound—was turned off. The air-conditioning machinery was switched off, lest its sound betray us. The whir of the fans ceased. The blowers stopped. The hydraulic pump jarred to a halt. The whine of the electric generators died away. The men took off their sandals lest a footfall betray us. In the galley the mess cooks silently shifted pots and pans from the stove to the floor, lest an accidental push send them clattering down.

Throughout the ship the buzz of conversation stopped. We waited. The heat began to increase. The *Wolf* was as silent as a tomb save for the low grind of my sound controls as I spun dials, worked my wheels frantically to keep the Jap clear in my phones. Now he was 5,000 yards away. I must know where he was every second and where he would be. The perspiration began to roll off me. It seemed as though someone was pouring water down my back. Four thousand yards ... three thousand ... two thousand ... one thousand ... The temperature within the *Wolf* was at least 110 degrees ... five hundred yards... I began to say, "Bearing two five five," but I never pronounced the second five. The first depth charge exploded. Everything suddenly turned upside down. It was the loudest sound I had yet heard. It was as solid as a blow on the skull, it was like a thunderclap between my ears. I found myself on the floor, my stool upturned. Maley was on the floor beside me, scrambling to his feet. We were in a snowstorm— paint chippings and cork from the bulkheads filled the air. The photographs of Marjorie and Spike tumbled down on me. The books on the shelf fell to the floor. Paint flew off corners. Overhead, electric bulbs shattered in their sockets. The lights flickered off, then on again. The wall opposite me billowed in toward me; the force of the concussion was so great it had contracted the *Wolf*'s hull like a rubber ball. It was as though a gigantic hand had reached under the sea, grabbed the *Wolf* about the middle, and shaken her.

I was sitting in a puddle of my own perspiration, one hand flung back to break my fall. I tried to get up. I reached forward to grab my bearing-control lever, and an electric shock jarred me from head to toe. I was grounded in my own sweat. I tingled to my fingertips. And all the time from that terrific explosion it seemed that somewhere, deep in my skull, behind my eyes, my brain pan jangled like a struck bell.

All this could have taken only a few seconds. As from a great distance I heard Captain Warder's voice, asking insistently, "Where is he now, Eckberg? Where is he now?"

I put my hands to my phones to adjust them and found them over my temples. I pushed the left phone over my ear—and another charge exploded. This was even closer than the first, right off the beam of the ship. I can hear today only because the phones were not on my ears. The *Wolf* lurched sharply. There was no screaming, no panic. I listened hard, balanced on the edge of the stool, and I caught the Jap screws again. He had passed our beam. He was going up our port side. He was driving up on the bow. I managed to call out his bearing.

"Good work, Eckberg," said the intercom. "Keep it up. Good work."

A moment later Captain Warder's voice came to me again, surprisingly clear. He had abandoned the conning tower and taken a stool in the control room just outside my shack. The conning tower had been sealed off. Now we could see each other if he leaned to the left and I to the right. Here he could talk directly to me, and from here he could control the *Wolf*'s activities.

A third depth charge landed. It wasn't as close. I could hear the Jap's propellers through it. Now more charges, each a little farther away. I was shouting bearings, and Captain Warder was snapping orders.

Our depth gauge had to tell us much. If a charge exploded above us, it drove us down. If the gauge showed eighty feet and a moment later one hundred feet, the charge had exploded above us. If we bounced up, it had exploded under us. The Jap was trying to land them so close that the concussion would rip open the *Wolf*'s seams. If he managed to explode one directly under us, we'd ride the bubble of air right to the surface, where he could finish us off with his deck guns.

"She's gone away, Captain," I finally announced.

The Skipper passed a hand over his forehead. He clenched and unclenched his left hand. "Dick," he said, "pass the word. Have the mess cooks run coffee through the ship for all hands."

Lieutenant Holden gave the word, and Gus Wright, undisturbed as always, came through with, "Who wants a cup of mud? Come and get it!"

We gulped down our coffee. And then the entire crew began digging into corners looking for leaks. Zerk and Dishman and Snyder were crawling about in grease and slime, and Zerk came crawling out of a corner with a grin to announce, "Well, she held together down here, anyway."

Dishman, who had No. 1 engine, would take no one's word that she was all right. He swarmed around her like a mother hen looking out for her brood, inspecting every nut and bolt, feeling, listening, watching.

Still submerged, we ran for the southern exit of the straits. We thought we had sunk two ships. We knew the *Wolf* had been hurt by the depth charges—probably not badly, but a few air and water lines had sprung small leaks, according to the report from the men crawling about. We wanted to reach the open sea to surface and recharge batteries, to examine the *Wolf*'s injuries, and to send a report to the High Command of what we had done.

We dared not use our transmitter in the straits because the Japs could put direction finders on us. Out at sea, by the time they determined where we were sending from, we'd be away from there with all the ocean to hide in. We remained down until well after dark. Jap planes were still in the area and probably working frantically to spot us. I maintained a continuous watch and heard no propellers over a two-hour period. Captain Warder took frequent periscope observations and reported nothing in sight. But we took no chances. These waters were phosphorescent. A submarine left a white wake easily seen from the air. Not until 9 p.m. did we rise slowly to the surface.

Now we worked hard. Our auxiliary gang under Zerk toiled all night repairing the leaks. I sent off my dispatch reporting our action and the damage incurred. We recharged batteries. Then we turned in our tracks and headed back full speed for Lombok Straits. We weren't finished with the Japs by a long shot. This time the Skipper chose a new route, to protect himself against a possible ambush. Instead of proceeding around the left side of Nusa Besar, as before, he came around the right, and then the *Wolf* dove directly in front of the island. We spent from dawn until noon fighting the currents to get into a position to attack the Japs if they were still where we'd seen them the day before.

Captain Warder peered through the periscope. Nothing. No ships in sight. We scanned the sea endlessly all that day and found no trace of the Japs. Later we learned that they failed to make that landing on Bali that day and the *Wolf* was credited with having repelled it. We patrolled for two days in and out of the straits. We heard the Japanese version of what we'd done off Bali the second night when we tuned in Radio Tokyo. The English voice was contemptuous:

"Our fleet has again shown its superiority over the Allied submarines." (Snickers from us.) "In a recent landing on the Island of Bali"—(More snickers)—"our forces ran into a nest of Allied submarines. The advantages went to our fleet forces. We destroyed—"

"By Christ," exclaimed Sousa, "we're a whole nest of them, you know that?"

"—several of the enemy and not one of his submarines was able to accomplish a successful attack. This type of warfare is becoming more and more successful. It will not be long until we have eliminated the last Allied submarine from Pacific waters."

Zerk commented, "Well, probably they have sunk a lot of our boats we don't know about."

Sousa glared at him. Lieutenant Deragon said, "You see the kind of fairy tales they're putting out? How are they going to win the war by putting out stuff like that for home consumption?"

John Street, with his score card, just grinned.

After that depth charging, the crew of the *Wolf* seemed more closely knit together than before. Maley and I particularly seemed to hit it off well. Even though one of the sound shafts was out of commission, neither of us felt at ease in action after that unless we both were in the shack.

Now we patrolled constantly. We had several uneventful days. We remained submerged during the daylight hours, surfaced at night, recharged batteries, then waited for dawn, hoping each day would bring us a target. One night a message came for us to keep out of the straits from dusk until dawn. A Dutch raiding party of cruisers and destroyers was coming through. The following night, lying off the straits in the position assigned to us, we had a box seat for the show. Frank Franz, bridge lookout at the time, told me later that he saw flashes of gunfire and the flare of bursting shells. Apparently our Dutch friends met a Jap raiding party in the middle of the night and sank four or five Jap ships.

A little later another urgent dispatch: a Jap convoy had been sighted, was on such and such a course.

When the convoy struck the center of the straits we were there, waiting. Captain Warder again determined the point where he thought the Japs would attempt to land. We waited for the false dawn, when a submarine commander has good visibility, but it is difficult to detect his periscope a few inches above the water.

The *Wolf* dove at 4:30 a.m. We hadn't sighted the convoy yet. It was a moonless night. As soon as we got down and leveled off, however, I heard the familiar *ping! ... ping! ... ping!* There they were! On the alert.

Now Captain Warder exhibited the most skillful maneuvering I've ever seen. By sound we were able to determine that eight ships were coming toward us, four in single file and two each on either side as escorts. Obviously, the four in single file were troop transports; their screws labored through the water. The other four were destroyers. Their screws beat with a cleaner, quicker beat. By sound alone Captain Warder maneuvered the *Wolf* to a point he sought between the two leading transports. In that position he could fire all of our torpedoes in rapid succession and with maximum damage to the enemy. It was as clear-cut as a problem in geometry.

"Yes, here they are!" Captain Warder announced at the periscope. "This is a real landing force. They've probably got them packed in there like sardines ... Are the tubes ready?"

The word came back: "All tubes ready, sir."

The *Wolf* waited.

"Stand by ... Fire!"

Now, in order, the *Wolf* sent torpedoes crashing into the two leading transports. Without waiting for the result, the Skipper swung his periscope around, got the first destroyer in the cross-hairs of the object glass, and barked: "Fire!"

A series of explosions shook the *Wolf* as our fish crashed into the three ships. I heard screws.

"We hit all three," came Captain Warder's jubilant voice.

76

"Here come the others. Those other three destroyers are making a beeline for us. Down periscope. Take her down! Rig for depth-charge attack! ... Dammit .." His voice trailed away. "I'd have liked to see those three babies sink!"

We went down. We wondered how bad this would be. Then the screws began pounding in my ears. Here was one set of high-speed screws, and then another, and then a third. Now I had too many to keep track of: they were coming and going in all directions. Although we were shaken up by their depth charges, no great harm was done. But they were persistent. We were depth charged intermittently, and not until noon did we hear the last of them. We waited. The heat began to increase again. When we'd been submerged for hours, the Skipper upped periscope for a swift glance about.

The nearest ship was 8,000 yards away. Captain Warder raised approximately six inches of periscope above the water—and damned if the Jap didn't see it, from that distance of more than four miles!

"Down periscope! He's started to head this way," exclaimed the Skipper. "I don't know if he saw us or not. I don't see how he could have from that range. I'll take another look to be sure."

The periscope slid up again. Captain Warder had it above surface less than five seconds.

"Down periscope! He *has* seen us!"

The Skipper turned around. His voice was louder. "Do you know," he said, "I saw men all over that ship. They were hanging on the masts and on every piece of superstructure, and every man had a pair of binoculars!" He added, "I'm taking no more chances with the periscope. Sound, what's he doing?"

I could hear the Jap clearly. "I have a bearing, Captain. He's bearing one nine zero, steady bearing."

"Good! Keep track of him. Let me know everything."

The Jap screws grew louder. They were drawing dead astern. My heart was in my mouth.

"Captain!" I yelled. "He's coming and he's coming fast, and he's going to come right over us!"

The *Wolf* was as still as a grave. Now every man in the ship, standing at his post, his heart beating fast, listening with all his might, heard the propellers of the destroyer reach a roar, fill all space with sound, pass over—and then go on.

There was not much water between the stool upon which I sat tense and the keel of the Japanese destroyer. And not a depth charge was dropped. Later Captain Warder analyzed what must have happened. A Jap lookout sighted our periscope, but reported it simply as an "object"—not a periscope. The destroyer sped over to investigate. His course was so true that he passed directly over us.

The heat was beginning to tell now. In the maneuvering space it had reached 140 degrees. The air was foul with the odor of human bodies. We dripped with perspiration. Captain Warder ordered saline tablets distributed, and Doc Loaiza, whose beard now made him look more like a Turk than a Puerto Rican, for it framed his mouth in a perfect black oval, passed them out.

When he came by, his feet squelched in perspiration, almost half an inch thick on the deck. A messboy brought in a gallon jug of water. I lifted the jug to my lips, drank, and spit it out. It had become brackish. It had a coppery taste from the lining of the water tank. Repeated tossing about had stirred up the sediment. It wasn't fit to drink. Maley sat beside me, naked to the waist, mopping his body with a soaked undershirt. The pressure in the boat was high from the compressed air we'd sucked back each time we fired a fish. The air-conditioning had been off so long the heat had reached a terrific point.

Captain Warder, sitting in his chair, perspiration pouring off him, asked repeatedly, "Anything on sound now, Eck?"

Each time I reported, "I can still hear them, sir, but nothing very close."

My watch over, I lurched across the control room, through the passageway, bumping against the bulkheads, and climbed heavily into my bunk. It grew hotter. I lay there, trying to breathe, as gently and as little as possible.

At last Captain Warder dared to take another periscope observation. He saw nothing. And finally the *Wolf* rose to the surface.

The *Wolf* had been submerged for long hours, and for most of that time with her air-conditioning off and under the cumulative air pressure of the compressed air sucked back in the firing of eight torpedoes.

The hatch was opened. As if produced by magic, a small gale roared through the ship. Papers flew about. The clothes of the men standing in the passageway billowed outward; their hair stood on end as though they had touched an electrically charged rod. The foul air imprisoned under pressure in the *Wolf* was rushing out the hatch, and they were in its path. The Diesels started up: the gale was reversed; fresh air poured in.

The men breathed deep draughts. They began to talk again. "Doesn't that stuff smell good!" and "Oh, God, it does!" Then, laughter. "Well, goddammit, we gave them hell and we got away with it, didn't we?" And, "I'll bet we can hear those slant-eyed bastards hissing all the way over here!"

Captain Warder wasted no time. The *Wolf* headed directly out to sea. Once more we inspected our damage and sent a report of our action. This time damage was practically nil. We all managed to get a good night's sleep.

Next morning, refreshed, we headed into the straits again. We had got three Jap ships, and we wanted more. But we could find nothing. Apparently we'd frightened them off again.

On the fourth night my radio spluttered with an order from the High Command to leave the area and start a new patrol.

We had been out for some time now, and our new patrol was an area off Tjilatjap, a Javanese seaport on the south coast used by the Allied powers to evacuate personnel from the East Indies to Australia. Hours before we reached our position we saw the city aflame. The flames lit up the sky for miles around.

Bridge lookouts told us the shoreline looked like a carnival of light and fire. Only the pillars of black smoke twisting furiously upward told the story. The Dutch, following the scorched-earth policy, were putting the torch to everything before the Japs arrived.

For several days we made routine patrols, watching the burning city, and waiting for the Japs to show up and pluck off their prize. Then a new dispatch ordered us into the southern entrance of Sunda Straits, a 60-mile-wide stretch of sea between Sumatra and Java. If the Japs hoped to reach the southern coast of Java in their southward push, they must use the Sunda Straits. Our job was to sink anything they'd try to send through. We had perfect conditions in these waters, which were deep and maneuverable, and Captain Warder and Lieutenant Deragon spent hours poring over their chart tables, plotting out the probable shipping lanes the Japs would use.

"I think we can ignore the Sumatra side," Captain Warder's voice said. "I don't see anything there. But the Java side does have a beautiful harbor. They might try to put some ships in there." He added, "But we can't get up there because of the water depth." And finally: "Very well, Willie, this is the way we'll do it: We'll run back and forth on a coastal patrol for several days. If we haven't made any contacts by that time, we'll set a patrol to take us into the center of the straits."

We spent quite a few days there, and saw nothing but the wreck of a Jap bombing plane. It was a long patrol, made under the constant strain of expectation, and for the first time an attack of nerves broke out. Half a dozen men weren't talking to one another. By this time we had been out on the longest sustained run we had made so far—and most of the crew had not seen the sun or been topside all during the patrol. It didn't help any that we were all running short of cigarettes. There were less than half a dozen packs left on the boat. Some of the men had a few cigars, and they nursed these along. Those who smoked pipes weren't in any better fix. Their tobacco was all gone. There were some pretty stretched tempers on the *Wolf*.

Then came a dispatch from the High Command ordering us to patrol the Christmas Island area and then proceed to a southern port.

Heading for port! That meant a new lease on excitement for all of us. We hopped to it. Christmas Island was a little piece of British land south and west of Java, valuable for its phosphate. It was John Street, with his gift for looking up things, who checked on the place and discovered it was an old pirate hangout. O.K., we thought. We'd do a little pirating ourselves.

We started immediately, diving by day and surfacing by night. At dawn of the third morning we were in a perfect position to dive off the island. Captain Warder took pains. The Allies were reported still in possession of the island and to have established batteries on shore. These batteries had spotted a couple of reconnoitering Jap subs and were presumed to have sunk them. We had to be careful: from a distance all submarines look alike.

The Skipper could find no sign of life. Our charts indicated that the only dock facilities on the island were in a small inlet called Flying Fish Cove. The Skipper found the cove and kept a wary eye on it.

"I ought to go in there tonight and blow that dock up," I heard him say. "The Japs probably will have it, anyway."

"Might be a good idea," came Ensign Mercer's voice.

Captain Warder hesitated. "But there are probably some natives on the island. They may be killed on the docks."

Nothing was done. That night we received a coded dispatch:

"Air reconnaissance shows transports, destroyers, and cruisers en route to Lombok Straits."

Apparently the convoy was bound for Christmas Island. *Well,* my thoughts ran, *if anyone can keep us out of harm, this man will do it. He's an artist with a submarine.*

"What I want to do," the Skipper was saying, "is to put your direction finder on this frequency and keep searching. Be sure you cover it thoroughly. I want you to sweep over your entire range of frequency constantly."

With action in sight, petty quarrels vanished. Men spoke to each other again. Stations were checked and then double checked. It was as though an electric shock had gone through the crew. We patrolled all day. We saw nothing. I searched and searched and searched.

"They're probably coming in under cover of darkness," said the Skipper.

At night we surfaced. At dawn we dove in front of Flying Fish Cove. The Japs had the same charts as we, and undoubtedly they'd set their course for the cove. With their heavier armaments they might bombard the island before attempting a landing, trying to knock out the shore batteries.

Captain Warder tirelessly studied his charts. He analyzed the Jap strategy: "The cruisers will bombard the island, with the transports undoubtedly standing off, waiting for the bombardment to cease. In that case the destroyers will be used to guard against submarines. That means our most valuable targets are the cruisers. Very well, we'll ignore the destroyers. We'll attack the transports if conditions are favorable, and we'll really make a try for the cruisers."

When we surfaced that night we found a brilliant moon flooding the sea. We dared not be silhouetted against it. We went out to sea and recharged batteries. Beginning at dawn, Captain Warder made periscope observations. Our intercom system was open. We waited tensely. At the 7:30 a.m. observation came Captain Warder's voice saying sharply:

"Here they are! *Ummmm.* Four cruisers in a line. Bombarding formation. I believe they're going to shell the island. Stand by to mark these bearings down, Casler. First cruiser, mark ..."

Rudy Gervais, at the helm, spoke up: "One seven two, sir," he said, giving the *Wolf*'s course, reading clockwise from true north.

Captain Warder: "Three four two," giving the course of the first cruiser.

Ensign Casler, thus having the cruiser's course and the *Wolf*'s course, could determine the angle between and use this to compute our approach.

"Second cruiser, mark," came Captain Warder's voice. "Three three nine ... Third cruiser, mark ... three four seven ... Fourth cruiser, mark ... three five two."

Casler meanwhile had been taking down not only the figures but the time each mark had been made. The *Wolf* now knew the courses of the four Jap cruisers in relation to our own course.

"Well, now," said Captain Warder, still at the periscope, "put this down. These are light cruisers, probably with six-inch guns. They carry planes. Two turrets forward. Turret aft. Catapults. I believe torpedo tubes. Typical Jap bow. Raked stern. Fire control tower is typical Japanese. Pagoda style. Got all that, Casler?"

"I have it all down, sir."

"All right .... Lovely day for our side .... I've got a good chop up here .... Beautiful for periscope work. Here's an approximate range: 12,000 yards. Angle on the bow, I'd say about eighty starboard. Speed, about thirteen knots. Casler, let's see what we can do with that. Down periscope."

A moment later: "I think I'll have another look at those babies. Up periscope." A pause of perhaps forty seconds. "Well, the transports are heading for Flying Fish Cove. Apparently the island has been abandoned. At least, they're not firing. I'd certainly like to get in an attack on those transports, but we're too far out. But these destroyers aren't too far off. Here's a bearing on that nearest one. Mark."

Rudy's voice: "One seven two, sir."

Captain: "Two eight four." This cruiser was just off our port beam. "Down periscope. Sound, do you have any of those propellers down there?"

I was on the alert. "I have that last cruiser you mentioned, Captain."

The Skipper set the *Wolf*'s course to intercept the four cruisers. During the next hour he took frequent bearings on the Jap men-of-war. Finally, "Up periscope." Then, "Mark!" His voice was several notes higher. He sounded like a hound near the rabbit. "Cruiser Natori class. Angle on the bow, five starboard. Range, 3,000. Seems to be making medium speed. Down periscope."

"Zero zero three, Captain," announced Casler. The cruiser was coming toward us almost head-on—only three degrees away from a collision course.

Suddenly, "Battle stations!" the *aaaap! ... aaaap!* blared through the boat. The crew moved swiftly and silently into place.

"Battle stations are manned, sir," reported Lieutenant Holden, diving officer.

"Good!" said Captain Warder. "Up periscope ... This ship is patrolling. His planes are still on the deck. Down periscope. Range, 2,300. Left full rudder. Ahead two-thirds. Come to course three four zero."

We were all tense now. I gave the Skipper bearings every few minutes. We were using every device we had to get into position for the kill. "Up periscope," came the Captain's voice. "Ah!" he said. "I see a command pennant. The admiral of this little organization is aboard this baby. Down periscope." He added, "Tell the forward room to make ready the tubes."

"Forward room. Make ready the tubes," came from the Captain's talker. Then: "Captain, forward room has the word, sir."

"Very well." Captain Warder turned to Mercer. "This fellow doesn't know we're here," he said. "He's not zigging. If he keeps coming ... Sound, have you got him?"

I had him. "Bearing three five two, Captain."

"Yes, that's about where he should be," commented the Skipper. "Stay on him, Eckberg ... Now, let's take another look. Wait a minute ... Willie, are you all set down there? How does it look?"

Lieutenant Deragon replied: "Everything checking so far, Captain."

"Very well. Open the outer doors."

Moments passed. The word came echoing back: "Outer doors open, sir."

"Up periscope," ordered Captain Warder. "Now, the usual method of firing, Willie. All set?"

"All set, Captain." Lieutenant Deragon's voice was steady.

"All set, Henry?"

"All set, Captain." Henry Bringelman, at the firing controls, spoke as calmly as though he were giving the weather report.

"Okay," said the Captain. He put his eye to the periscope. "Here he is. Stand by ... stand by ... Fire one!"

I caught the sound of the fish as she went. My ears clicked with the sudden increase in air pressure.

"One fired, sir!"—this from Bringelman, below.

"Stand by, two ... stand by ... Fire two!"

And almost like an echo, Bringelman's deep voice: "Torpedoes fired, sir."

I heard the high-pitched whines. "The fish are running, Captain," I sang out.

"That's fine, Eckberg. They're hot, eh?"

"Yes, sir. Straight and hot."

A second's pause. "Number three hit," came the Skipper's voice. "She's slowing down. Her propellers are still turning over. There go the steam jets! ... There's panic on her! Men running all over the ship! Dammit, I'd sure like to see one of those babies sink just once! Oh, oh, here they come. Take her down!" His voice faded. "Let's get out of the conning tower," he said. "Eckberg, you're going to have four sets of screws coming at you. They're coming here like a bat out of hell." He raced down the ladder into the control room to take his place on the chair outside my shack. The conning tower was sealed off. We had only a few minutes to wait. I picked up the screws. They were coming up the starboard side very fast.

Now the depth charges came. They were coming viciously, one every ten or fifteen seconds, beautifully spaced. They came nearer and nearer our starboard side, and it seemed impossible that one wouldn't get us. I thought we were lost. The ship shuddered and rocked. The radio shack was again filled with a blizzard of flying paint and cork. Locker doors swung open and clanged shut again. I managed to hold to my stool this time, and turned just in time to see the cans of dynamite tumbling across the deck. I stuck out my foot and held them under it. The breath was almost knocked out of me, but I gave the Skipper every bearing I could. I shouted at the top of my voice. Captain Warder wasn't seated now, he was standing, clinging and swinging with the heaving of the *Wolf*. Every time I shouted bearings, he shouted back, "Good! Good! Good! That's fine! Keep it up!"

His eyes were glued to the depth gauge. We were bouncing up and down like a rubber ball. The first screws died out of my phones; another set came in. *Oh, God, I thought, now it begins all over again!* One destroyer had completed his run of depth charges, and a second was coming up the portside to repeat the depth charging on that side. They were out to get us. I stole a swift glance at Paul. He was holding on for dear life, but he had a pencil in his hand and a pad before him, and he was a tally sheet on the charges. Four vertical lines, and then one through, for every five ... Intermittently, all through that day, the *Wolf* was depth charged. The explosions churned the sea about us. Every man was alert at his station. There was no sleep. And somehow we escaped unhurt.

Late that night we surfaced, and then all night we dodged the same brilliant moon that harassed us the night before. We had to remain approximately fifteen miles off shore. The crew was in fine fettle. We were doing all right. We actually skipped sleep to take turns crowding about the conning tower ladder to breathe the fresh air and gloat over the damage we'd done. In Kelly's Pool Room the men were tired but jubilant. Gus Wright was sitting at a table, a cup at his side, his brows knit, and I would have sworn he was rolling a cigarette. Where did he get the tobacco and paper? I looked closer. The paper was toilet tissue. The tobacco ...

"Coffee grounds," said Gus seriously. "I've been drying them in the oven." He held the paper in his left hand, sprinkled the black grounds into it from the cup, smoothed them out with a practiced hand, rolled it, flicked it across his tongue—and he had a cigarette. He lit it up and began to smoke. "Had to do this once when I ran a sheep drive up to Oregon," he said, and winked.

I like my cigarettes, but not that bad. I'd got my fresh air. I went forward and hit the sack for a fifteen-minute nap.

When the moon went down that morning, the *Wolf* turned toward the island again. It was about 2 a.m. We were making slow speed. Slowly we drove toward the enemy. It would take us until dawn to get to the point at which the Captain wanted to be. At 4 a.m. we had reached a spot eleven miles from shore, when suddenly:

"Clear the bridge! Stand by to dive!" It was Lieutenant Syverson on the bridge.

Captain Warder, in his pajamas, raced into the control room. The diving alarm sounded. We were under in a matter of seconds. By the time we leveled off, I knew we had spotted a ship on the port quarter. We didn't think he'd seen us. I took over sound and located him in one minute. Through the intercom Captain Warder said, "They're really looking for us if they're this far out. What do you hear, sound?"

"I've got him. Captain," I said. "He's over on the port beam now. Not making much speed."

Captain Warder upped periscope. It was dawn. "I see him," he said a moment later. The Jap couldn't see our periscope. We were very careful now. We were running out of torpedoes. We had only a couple of attacks left in us. "I'll be damned!" came the Skipper's voice at the periscope. "This cruiser is similar to the one we hit yesterday." He peered again. "And damned if they haven't a command pennant flying." He chuckled. "Boys, did we shift that Admiral around, or are they trying to trick us?"

Finally, we attacked. We fired at 5:13 a.m.

"Can you hear them run, Eckberg?" came the familiar question.

Their whine was clear under the steady beating of the Jap's screws. What I wanted to hear was that explosion, and the sudden silencing of those screws.

"Yes, sir, I hear them. I hear them, all right."

"I believe they're heading straight for the target," the Skipper said.

Suddenly the *Wolf* jarred.

"We smacked her!" exclaimed the Skipper. "Let's go."

I heard the death rattle of the Jap ship in my phones. It is an unmistakable symphony of death you hear as a torpedoed ship slowly sinks at sea. First, a series of sharp reports, like a string of firecrackers set off—her ammunition exploding. Then two muffled explosions, almost simultaneously—the cold water has reached her steam boilers, and they have blown up. With that, the sudden halting of the steady *whish—sh ... whish—sh ... whish—sh* of the screws, broken off sharply, like a voice suddenly choked off. Now fugitive crackling, splintering little explosions—the ship's pipes breaking up, her plates buckling and twisting off, and all this time, a slow, hollow gurgling like a man dying ... A few seconds of complete silence. Then the final *Whoomph!*—the ship's hull caving in like an eggshell between pile drivers as she reaches a depth where the water pressure is overwhelming. In that final *Whoomph!* everything gives way at once.

"She's gone, Captain," I said.

"Good!" said the Skipper. He trained his periscope on the sea where the ship had been. "I don't see a damn thing," he said. "No debris. Nothing at all. Are you sure you heard the screws stop, Eckberg?"

"Yes, sir. I heard her blow up, Captain."

"You're probably right," he said. "I can't see a trace of her up here. I think we really smacked her in the right place. I don't think there are any survivors from this one."

I glanced at my watch: 5:17 a.m.

The ship with all hands had gone down in little more than three minutes flat.

Captain Warder spoke directly to the torpedo room. "Thank you, boys. Nice work, after torpedo room. Nice work on those bearings, sound."

Five minutes later I picked up a set of high-speed screws. I reported it.

"Oh, yes," said the Captain. "Sure, they'll be along to see what happened to their buddies. They're going to be awfully baffled. Let's see ..." He looked through the periscope again. "Yes, here they are. I can see them using their searchlights. They won't find anything. Down periscope. I don't want those big searchlights to swing around and spot us."

The Jap destroyers paid their respects with two mild depth charges. We scarcely noticed them. We secured battle stations and returned to Flying Fish Cove.

As the morning went on, we spotted a few ships. The crew was still on the alert. Nothing happened. Toward noon, the Skipper took another periscope observation near the cove entrance.

"Ah," he said. "They're getting ready to leave. Yes, the Nips are engaged in some very intense anti-submarine patrols. Here are destroyers patrolling ..." His voice rose. "Here is a cruiser launching a plane. Boy, they really are looking for us. Down periscope. Dammit, I'd like to get in that water right at the cove mouth, but it's as flat as a pancake, and they'd pick me up. There's no doubt they're getting ready to leave. I can see the transports moving around inside the cove. What they're probably doing is sweeping for us right now. Do you hear them pinging, Eckberg?"

"Yes, sir," I sang out. "Three or four pingers, sir, all over the place."

"That's what I thought," he said. "They're worried and want to get out. They're a bit scared about leading those transports out. That means the cruisers and cans will sweep this place thoroughly before any mass movement begins. I did see one cruiser angling over this way, though. ... If he would keep coming we might get in this last attack." His voice suddenly changed. "Thompson, have them make ready that last torpedo and let me know when that's done."

"Aye, aye, sir," came Thompson's voice.

"Sound, do you hear anything new?"

"About the same, Captain," I reported. "That cruiser you spotted is still coming this way. Pretty steady bearing, too."

"Is that so?" commented the Skipper. "Well, let's take a look. Thompson, as soon as that fish is ready, have them open the outer doors."

"Aye, aye, sir," came Thompson's voice promptly.

"Up periscope," said the Captain. *"Ummmmm.* Yes, here he is. We can't close with him, though. If he'd zig this way a little ... No, he's going to get by us, dammit! I certainly would like to take a crack at him. Wait a minute ... He is zigging—and this way, too! Put this down ... Bearing, mark!"

"Two six five," came Rudy's voice.

Captain Warder looked at his azimuth. "Three two zero," he said. "Estimated range, 3,000. Angle on the bow, ninety starboard. Give me a normal approach in a hurry. Is that fish ready, Thompson?"

"Fish is ready and outer doors are open, Captain," responded Thompson.

"Right full rudder," ordered the skipper. "What's that approach course, Casler?"

"Three zero zero, Captain," said Casler, who'd been working it out on the plotting table.

"That's fine," said the skipper, his eyes still at the periscope. "Rudy, come to three zero zero ... He's still coming this way. Down periscope." In a satisfied voice, "We'll fire on the next observation. Sound, have you got him?"

"I got him, Captain."

"Good! Let me know if he changes course or speeds up. This baby has a pennant, too. Well. If we sink him, that Admiral will have to get on one of those destroyers."

There was snickering audible all through the boat.

"All right," said Captain Warder briskly. "Let's have a look. Up periscope." Pause. "My ... what a target! I can't wait. Stand by ... ready, Hank?"

"Ready, sir," came Hank's deep voice.

"Fire!" Captain Warder's order was sharp.

Our last torpedo shot from the *Wolf*'s bow. I followed it right to the target. It was a perfect hit, but I knew we dare not stick around to see her sink.

"Now," said Captain Warder dryly, "if we had a few more fish we could have this Admiral riding a canoe. He doesn't have many more cruisers left here. All right, now. Abandon conning tower. Rig for depth charges. They'll be coming around again."

It was 4 p.m. We knew this was going to be a tough one. The Japs—partly in panic, partly in rage—would make us remember this. We were not wrong. Most of us had not had any sleep for nearly thirty-six hours. We had now been under for a long time, and the moment the air-conditioning was turned off we began to feel the heat and closeness. The humidity was very high. We waited for the worst, Captain Warder, wearing only shorts like the rest of us, sitting in his chair outside the sound shack.

The next hours were hell. At the beginning I heard the Jap's screws coming toward us. I picked the loudest and ignored the others. I stuck to him. After the second hour, the heat, the closeness, the strain, the lack of sleep began to tell. We found it difficult to carry out routine orders. I found myself repeating Captain Warder's words to myself for fear I would forget the first words by the time I heard the last. It was difficult to concentrate. Our minds worked sluggishly. After the fourth hour, a fog of moisture and humidity settled in the compartments throughout the *Wolf.* We squinted at each other. Some of the men lay sprawled on their bunks, seeking to conserve their strength. Others slumped on stools, their shirts tied about their waists to keep perspiration from running down their naked bodies.

I was leaning on my elbow on the plate glass of my desk, and once, glancing down, saw that my perspiration had run down the glass and into the blue blotter I had placed under it, soaking the blotter and dripping from it, as from a soggy cloth, onto the linoleum deck, already swimming in perspiration. The sweat was rolling down my elbows in streams. The skin of my hands was pinched and white. I found myself nervously rubbing my palms against my knees, kneading the dirt out.

The stench in the *Wolf* grew unbearable. It was salty, and acrid, and nauseating, made up of perspiration, oil, staleness, and oven-like heat. Few of us had to answer any call of nature. Fear seemed to constrict our bowels, turn our stomachs into hard knots. Our bodies threw off such quantities of liquid that there was little for our kidneys to do. It was just as well. Our toilet tanks could not be emptied lest the air bubbles give us away on the surface. By 7 p.m. some of the men lay in their bunks near exhaustion. They tried to read, but the words swam before their eyes. The refrigerator had been switched off. Our drinking water was warm. Some of the men drank anyway and became nauseated. Doc Loaiza stumbled through the passageway, groping his way along the bulkheads, passing out saline tablets. They gagged us.

Once, during this time, Captain Warder stuck his head through the door of the sound shack. He whispered. I didn't get his words. I wondered why he was whispering. He repeated them. Then I understood. *How was I doing?* I wanted to show him I was at ease.

"I'm fine, Captain," I said, loudly—but my voice was a whisper, too. The pressure had become so great that your words literally stopped moving the moment they left your lips. They hung in the thick air. When orders came, they had to be squeaked from one man to the next.

Finally Captain Warder ordered the *Wolf* taken to periscope depth. We had to surface soon. The men needed air. The lights were dim; the batteries had to be recharged, for when they went down completely, we'd have to surface—or die.

"I see a destroyer over there," came the Skipper's hoarse voice at the periscope. And after what seemed an age: "He's waiting, all right. He's listening for us. Let's go back down."

Slowly the *Wolf* descended. Maley's face was gaunt as he slumped at my side. His cheeks were beaded with perspiration.

His eyes were red-rimmed. My beard was wet and sodden. It itched horribly. An inch of sweat swirled on the deck under my feet. I sat there, in a half stupor, when suddenly I felt myself tilting back on my stool. An empty can of Maley's pipe tobacco skidded off its shelf. *Hell, we were taking a terrific up-angle...*

Something was wrong. I jumped up and out into the control room. Everyone there was frozen at his place, eyes glued to the depth gauge. The needle was climbing down ... We were going up!

"Jesus, we're broaching!"

I was numb. After the punishment we'd taken, this was the end of everything. We were surfacing, showing ourselves, and the Japs were up there, waiting ...

Captain Warder slid down the control-room ladder. His feet hit the deck.

"Use negative!" he roared.

The crew leaped to positions. On nerve alone they stood and toiled with valves and controls and huge wheels, their sweat-glazed eyes on the depth gauge with its needle swinging lower, lower ...

There was a scream of escaping air. Water rushed into the *Wolf*'s gigantic emergency tank.

But we were still going up—up. I could hardly keep my feet. I grabbed a handle.

"For Christ's sake," a high-pitched voice screamed, "the conning tower's out. They can see us!"

"All ahead, emergency!" Captain Warder's voice was electrifying. "Bow-planes, sternplanes, hard dive!"

The *Wolf*'s powerful motors burst into an ear-splitting whine. She drove forward like a catapult. We waited, breathlessly. We had done all we could. If she surfaced now, it was out of our hands.

Slowly the needle began to climb. Slowly the *Wolf* checked her rise and began her descent. But for the moment we had to forget everything and save our lives again. The *Wolf* was gathering momentum now, plunging toward the bottom so swiftly she might reach depths so great the water pressure would cave in her sides. We had to stop her plunge downward as swiftly as we had stopped the plunge upward.

"Blow negative!" Captain Warder shouted. Air shrieked into the emergency tank, forcing the water out again. "All back, emergency!" We were reversing our propellers, we were giving ourselves away again to the enemy, sending air bubbles to the surface ...

If ever the *Seawolf* seemed destined to meet her end, this was the moment.

Ba-room! The first depth charge came over. With it the *Wolf* seemed to split up inside. Before my eyes the bulkheads billowed inward, then returned to their original position. The huge radio and sound gear, 800 pounds of panel and tubes and machinery, swayed like a drunken man. Water swished and churned madly through the superstructure over my head. In the engine room men were swept from their feet. And thrown from side to side, hurled from one bulkhead to the other, with wood and metal crashing and splintering about us, my mind went round and round like a broken record playing over and over again, *"Where is he, where is he, there he is, there he is, O God, there he is, there goes another, is that the last, is that the last ...?"*

Then, for a little while that seemed an age we waited at our stations, mouths dry, gasping, in air so foul, so thick, you could almost feel it in your hands. It was dusk in the world above us. Somehow the word came through. We had broached because somebody misinterpreted an order. Someone had blown too much water out of our bow tank. We went deeper now, and waited. I sat with my earphones, Maley at my side, and I trembled. Would I ever get out of this alive? We'd probably all be completely exhausted, every man helpless on his bunk now, if the broaching hadn't knocked us into alertness again. I looked up, and Lieutenant Deragon was in the doorway, looking at us. I must have looked pretty bad. He disappeared but was back in less than a minute.

"Here, Eckberg," he said, with a stony face. "You look as though you'll be needing this." He placed a roll of toilet paper beside me and vanished again.

That broke the tension. Maley and I grinned at each other.

"Remember those freighting days," Paul whispered. "Remember how we griped when we could sit around and play cards and argue about the news? Remember how we griped we were just carrying freight around ..." He coughed, and grinned again.

Captain Warder, the perspiration beaded in his eyebrows, deep lines in his face, looked in. "Eckberg, how much sleep have you had?"

"I don't know, Captain," I said. "I'm not very sleepy." I was so keyed up now I could have remained awake all night, I think.

The Skipper mopped his brow with a wilted handkerchief. It was Maley's watch coming up.

"I think we're going to stay down a little while longer," he said. "But most of the excitement is over. You'd better turn in and get some sleep."

"I don't think I can," I said. "I want to see us up and away so I can quit worrying."

The Skipper looked at both of us, and the corners of his mouth turned up in a tired smile. "All right," he said. "You boys have done a real job today. We'll get out of here and head for home now as soon as conditions permit. See that you get some sleep, Eckberg." And he was gone.

Somehow the time passed. Men with towels around their necks moved sluggishly with mops, swabbing the sweat from the decks, wringing the mops out into buckets. Buckets full of sweat stood in corners of the *Wolf*. Maley and I stewed in the radio shack. We alternated on the sound gear. We couldn't slow ourselves down.

It was nearly midnight when Captain Warder appeared again. "We're going to surface very shortly," he said wearily. "Take a good sweep all around and let me know what you hear."

I bent over my gear and searched. We knew it was black night up there, and that Captain Warder depended on sound to let him know what conditions were.

I must have spent ten minutes investigating every suspicious noise in every degree of the circle.

Finally I reported, "There's nothing up there as far as I can tell, sir."

"That's fine." His voice came hollowly from the conning tower. "All right, boys. Bring her up to periscope depth."

We rose slowly. Captain Warder upped his periscope. For fifteen minutes he scanned every inch of the horizon. I think it was the most concentrated scanning he had ever done. Then, his arms over the periscope crossbars, he turned. "Have the night lookouts come to the conning tower," he said.

The word was passed for the night lookouts. They climbed up.

"Boys," said the Captain, "I don't have to tell you to keep a sharp lookout tonight. I know you're tired, but this good air will revive you. Report anything at all suspicious." Then he ordered, "Surface!"

Three blasts of the horn, and up we went. At 1: 10 a.m. the hatch opened. The *Wolf* had been under for many hours and most of her crew had been without sleep for forty-three consecutive hours. The air roared through. A sudden chill made me shiver as I sat at my desk. Lieutenant Deragon came by again. He looked in. This time he grinned. Nothing ever seemed to upset him.

"Why don't you turn in, Eck?" he said. "We're O.K. now."

"I know," I said. And I asked him where we were. We were on our way to get around the point of the island, he said. "Let me show you," he added, and he led the way to the charts in the control room. He pointed out the route we were taking. We were going to a port in Australia. It was to be our new home port. "Here we are now," he said. "We turn at this point and head south."

"Where were we when we broached, sir?" I asked. He pointed that out. I said frankly, "I don't like it. We're not very far away from those destroyers."

"No," he said, "but we will be." He glanced at the speed indicator. "No, it won't be long now," he went on. "Anyhow, there's no use your staying up any longer. Turn in and get some sleep. You need it."

I said I wanted to stay up until we got around the corner, and so I did. First I sat down at radio and sent a long dispatch to the High Command, dictated by Captain Warder, recounting what had happened to us. Then I turned in.

When I awoke it was afternoon. I had slept fourteen hours. The *Wolf* was riding cautiously at periscope depth, on the alert for planes. Most of the crew were in their bunks, too, recuperating. They were too tired to talk. That night, after surfacing, we received a message from the High Command:

> *A wonderful cruise. Your accomplishments rank among the greatest of all time. Congratulations.*

Captain Warder had copies typed and posted conspicuously about the *Wolf.* The men clustered around the bulletin board in Kelly's Pool Room and read the Captain's personal PS:

TO ALL HANDS:

I want to take this opportunity to express my deepest thanks for your ability and your conduct, and above all, your devotion to duty. It is my firm hope that I will be with you all when we put out to sea on the next patrol.

Respectfully,

F. B. WARDER.

We knew the Japs had air supremacy in the Christmas Island area, and we proceeded cautiously toward Australia. Finally, one afternoon we were near enough to the Australian coast to surface in daylight. Captain Warder reported from the bridge, "It's a nice day ... A little cloudy. Choppy sea up here. We'll let a few of the boys come up."

I waited my turn. Frank Franz called down, "Got your dark glasses, Eck?"

I shouted up, "No. What do I need them for? It's cloudy up there, isn't it?"

"Sure," he said. "But that doesn't make any difference. You better wear those glasses." I was too anxious to go up. I had not been topside for many days and nights. I stopped at the entrance of the bridge. I shielded my eyes with my hands. "Permission to come on the bridge, sir?" I asked the officer of the deck.

It was Lieutenant Syverson. "Come ahead, Eckberg," he said.

I watched my feet as I moved up. Now, two steps to daylight. I lifted my hands, and lightning seared my brain. I clapped my hands over my tortured eyes. I saw red. My eyes burned as though I had been scalded. Hands over my eyes, now peering a bit, slowly I grew accustomed to daylight.

It was a beautiful day. Never had the sea seemed so blue, the whitecaps so white. My eyes drank in the glory of the sky and the open air. The smell of salt was so strong in my nostrils that I had a fit of sneezing. The taste of salt was in my throat. I stared at the other men as they came up. Their bodies, naked from the waist up, were an obscene white, like the white underbelly of a fish. Their faces were gray, like the faces of men taken out of dungeons. We discovered that only a few minutes on the bridge under that cloudy sky sunburned us. We discovered that none of us carried an ounce of excess weight. It was as though we had been in a Turkish bath, reduced and exhausted and dehydrated, days on end. When we finally climbed back into the depths of the *Wolf* again, we realized for the first time how foul the odor was. The air above made us dizzy when we came down. Our faces were flushed. We began to perspire. I lay down in my bunk for a twenty-minute rest after ten minutes in the air.

Our Australian port was only a few hours away, and it might mean our first mail since the war began. All the magazines we'd used to get at Manila might be waiting for us. But the mail! Word from home! We relaxed completely. We slept and ate—an orgy of fresh vegetables and milk and butter at the port was wonderful to look forward to—and went on deck every chance we had. We played our phonograph hour after hour. "The Five O'Clock Whistle" and "Melody in F" and swing and boogie-woogie sounded in Kelly's Pool Room day and night. We began breaking out our shore clothes. Men were pressing their dress blues all day long on the mess table. The ship's iron was hot twenty-four hours a day. For the first time in months we opened our razor cases. The blades were rusty and green with mold. Captain Warder relaxed, too. He resumed his setting-up exercises, a slender, bearded figure in shorts and sandals, taking deep breaths, flexing his muscles, counting to himself. In the afternoons he closeted himself in his stateroom and wrote out his reports—his war diary of the *Wolf*'s activities. Rudy Gervais accosted the Captain with an idea.

"Captain," he said, "how about us decorating our conning tower with Jap flags? We sunk a lot of ships."

The Skipper thought it over and said, "No, Rudy, I don't think that's a good idea. The *Seawolf* doesn't need flags up there. Everybody knows we sink ships. Let's not brag about it."

That disappointed some of the men. They liked the idea of having the *Wolf* come in with a broom upside down sticking out of the tower, or with some silhouettes of Jap men-of-war we'd sent down. But we had to admit that in sub circles everyone knew the *Wolf* did all right.

Finally the *Wolf* reached a prearranged rendezvous point, outside the port. Here a pilot came aboard and led us through the mine field guarding the entrance of the harbor. Then luck was with us. What we'd been waiting for—the bag of mail—was brought aboard. I grabbed a thick bundle of letters that bore my name and hurried into the sound room. Maley had his bundle and was reading them in his bunk.

I was so nervous I couldn't get the first envelope opened. I seemed all thumbs. But from the first one tumbled four snapshots. They were of Spike and Marjorie. I couldn't tear my eyes from them. I studied them over and over. Here was Spike in his carriage—the same Spike I had left, but much bigger. Here he was laughing in the sun—and behind him, Marjorie, looking the picture of health, smiling and wholesome and waiting for me. I felt like bawling. I read all the letters. Twenty-five of them, two from my brothers, twenty-three from Marjorie. She gave me a detailed picture of Spike. I followed him through each letter. He was a husky kid ... he hated that afternoon nap ... he was eating like a horse ... now he was grabbing the sides of the crib and trying to stand up by himself ... That hour made up for many things.

As we were about to glide into the harbor, another American submarine, Lieutenant Commander Lucius H. Chappell commanding, came into view. She had been out on a run and was returning to the dock. Captain Warder, who had never been in the port before, decided it would simplify matters to follow Captain Chappell in. He signaled him, "Go ahead, I'll follow you in."

The reply came back: "Congratulations, *Seawolf*. Proud to be with the record-breaker. After you, sir."

CHAPTER VII

"For Heroism ..."

FOR THE first time now we had a chance to get an overall look at the *Wolf*. She showed the punishment she had taken. Patches of her black paint had peeled off, and the bottom white showed through. Green moss, like a fantastic beard, flowed from her keel. The starboard side forward was peppered with shrapnel. Paint was chipped off the deck—testimony to the battering-ram action of depth charges. The mooring lines were swollen and rotting as they lay coiled in the sun.

At midday we found ourselves in a large channel clogged with ships. Warehouses flanked the docks, some of them so expertly camouflaged that we couldn't believe our eyes. We stood on deck and watched, and yearned for cigarettes. Captain Warder flashed a message to shore: "Please send out one case of cigarettes and twenty gallons of fresh milk." And soon a launch was bobbing alongside and the cigarettes were delivered. "Have at 'em boys," invited the Captain, and we all lit up. Captain Warder, his patrol report under his arm, left the ship. Now fresh fruit came aboard, apples and oranges. We grabbed them and began munching, and we talked about liberty. Someone said, "Shall we talk about women now or should we lead up to it gradually?" We were exhilarated. After a little while the Skipper returned, looking pleased. "Mr. Deragon, get them all to quarters," he said. "I have something to tell them."

We lined up in two ranks, still in our working dungarees. We must have been quite a sight: bearded and unkempt, our hair over our ears, some of us wiping grease off our hands with cotton waste.

"I have just come from the squadron commander," said Captain Warder. "I want to tell all you men that the entire High Command is pleased, exceptionally well pleased, with our performance. Needless to say, I feel the same way.

"I don't know how long we shall be here. It looks as though we'll have to undergo an extensive overhaul. That means a good rest for all of us. Now, when you go ashore, don't discuss any of our operations with anyone, even with your own shipmates. Leave the *Seawolf* tied down here. Don't drag her down into the city." He turned to Deragon. "Willie, anything you'd like to say?"

Deragon smiled. "Yes, sir, we are expecting the paymaster any minute." We all grinned. "Liberty will start immediately following pay day," Lieutenant Deragon went on. "It will expire at 7:30 a.m. aboard."

The paymaster came. We got our money. And as soon as we had the chance, we went over the side and made for a train that would take us into town, about four hours distant. We wanted to relax, take baths, take things easy, do everything we hadn't been able to do for so long, and to forget depth charges and heat and lack of sun.

Not all of us went off; the *Wolf* had to undergo extensive repair. The projector at the end of the No. 2 sound shaft had to be repaired. The entire area of the officers' staterooms, the starboard side and aft batteries, the galley and the scullery, had to be fixed up. But I was among those who went over first.

Among my first assignments to myself was a haircut and shave. I had a good two-inch beard. To my dismay I discovered that in Australia I'd be taken care of, not by a barber, but by a "hair-dresser." I went in and lay peacefully relaxed, while I was shaved and made presentable again. Suddenly I was slapped in the face with something icy cold. I almost jumped out of the chair. Then I learned that in Australia after a man is shaved a young boy comes about with a contraption which is a cross between an old-fashioned bellows and a fizz bottle. He stands off about four feet from you as you lie there expecting the barber to pat tingling after-shave lotion on your face, draws a bead—and shoots. This, it was explained to me, was a disinfectant.

From the beginning the crew of the *Wolf* was bath-crazy. Some of the men took three baths in a row. We ate, and washed, and showered and bathed. We couldn't get clean enough. Our feet pained at first; we had been so accustomed to sandals aboard the *Wolf* that even loose shoes pinched. The shoes led to a night's skylarking that almost had some embarrassing consequences. About a dozen of us were in a hotel in Perth one night and, according to custom, left our shoes outside our doors to be shined. The next morning I found a nicely shined pair of shoes outside my door—but instead of my size 12's, they were 8's. Then it developed that everyone had someone else's shoes outside his door. We were due back to the boat: we had to get back there. We dashed about, cursing, trying to match our shoes, and finally we all met in the lobby. Sully took charge, stood up on a desk, and auctioned off shoes according to size. As we were leaving, Sousa, looking pleased with himself, came down the stairs. He was wearing his own shoes. We didn't have time to cross-examine him then, but later, aboard the *Wolf*, he admitted all.

We dashed back to the boat. We poured over the gangplank, down into the *Wolf*, and, following orders, got on our dress blues. We hurried topside wondering what was up. Now it became even more puzzling. Word was passed through the ship that the High Command, headed by Rear Admiral Arthur S. Carpender, COMSUBSSOUWESTPAC—Commander of Submarines in the Southwest Pacific—was coming aboard with his staff. We thought he was coming to look the *Wolf* over, and we were mortified. She looked like a wreck. Sousa mustered us in forward of the conning tower, for the after-portion of the deck was so ripped up we couldn't stand there. We lined up, port and starboard side, Captain Warder and his officers directly in front of the conning tower, and in a few minutes the High Command boarded the ship. There was Admiral Carpender, a gray-haired, gimlet-eyed Navy veteran; Captain James Fife, Jr., whom we'd evacuated from Corregidor, now Chief of Staff, Submarines, Asiatic Fleet; Captain S. S. Murray; and other high officers. Everyone was stiffly at attention.

Admiral Carpender looked us over. "I congratulate you men on your magnificent achievement," he said. "You are the envy of every submarine in the Fleet. You've done a splendid and a memorable job, and we are proud of you. The cruise you have just completed has set a record for every other submarine to aim at." We all stood there, glowing. Then he turned to the Skipper. "Captain Warder," he said, crisply. The Skipper took two paces forward.

Admiral Carpender was holding a small leather case in his hand. Suddenly we all got it. They were going to decorate the Skipper! "Captain Warder," the Admiral was saying, slowly and distinctly, "you have been awarded the Navy Cross"—He paused. In the ranks we had to fight to keep from nudging each other and letting out a yell—"for heroism and especially meritorious conduct in combat with the enemy as Commanding Officer of this submarine in three separate engagements with heavy enemy Japanese Naval forces. Despite the extremely shallow and narrow waters, and the strong currents existing, you successfully attacked a large enemy screened force sinking one transport and one destroyer. Later you made repeated attacks upon heavily screened enemy light cruisers, sinking one cruiser and damaging two others."

He opened the case, took out the blue and white ribbon with its bronze Navy Cross, and, leaning over, pinned it over the Skipper's heart.

"I congratulate you, Captain," he said, and extended his hand. They shook hands warmly.

The crew of the *Wolf* was as thrilled as their Skipper. After all the congratulations were over and the High Command were gone, the Skipper turned to us.

"This cross is as much yours as it is mine, boys," he said earnestly. "You have contributed as much as, if not more than I to the earning of it. I'm proud of you all, and I'm proud of the *Wolf.*"

We stood about deck after he and the officers left, gazing at the torn-up *Wolf.* We were proud of her, too. She was a damn good boat. We'd a bone to pick with the High Command, though, about crediting us with those few ships. We'd done better than that, but we knew how conservative the Skipper was. Even Zerk, the pessimist, was burned up about that. As he went by the conning tower, he knocked on it with his knuckles three times. "They don't make 'em better than this baby," he said. And he said it for all of us.

Before we left there on our next mission of the war, the *Wolf* threw a party. Everyone was there, the High Command, the High Bishop of that area, who later visited the *Wolf* and gave the Captain, the ship, and her crew his blessing, and distinguished British, Australian, and American figures.

Then, a brief two-day stay at another Australian port, and the *Wolf* was off again. She'd only begun to fight!

CHAPTER VIII

Jinxed

WE LEFT port and headed north. A few nights later we pulled into a secret advance base where we fueled to capacity and filled our fresh-water tanks.

We had a guest aboard, a lieutenant commander. As part of his indoctrination period before taking over his own submarine, he was assigned to the *Seawolf* as an observer. He was pleasant, about thirty-five, kept to the wardroom, and was in no one's way. Yet a few of the old-timers grumbled. Some submarine men are convinced that strangers jinx a voyage.

This mission was clearly defined: unrestricted submarine warfare to destroy enemy shipping wherever encountered.

We caught our first target just below the port of Koepang, on the coast of Timor. We were heading up toward Dili, Timor, not far from the shore, when suddenly a night lookout spotted a coal-burning tramp steamer, a single-stacker, about 250 feet long, lumbering along at six knots. It was a perfect setup, so perfect we'd make a surface attack. There was a moon out, and the steamer was beautifully silhouetted against it. The sea was smooth. We were almost invisible, the *Seawolf*'s dark hulk blending into the background of beach, so that the small portion of her above water was almost impossible to detect.

I picked up the tramp's screws on sound. Now, very carefully, Captain Warder inched the *Wolf* into a position to fire. The orders came ... "Fire!"

I picked up their high whine. I watched the hand of my stopwatch tick away the seconds, waiting for the familiar *ka-rumphf* of the fish going home, or the muffled blast of the boilers exploding.

Nothing. We'd missed her. Slow and unhurried, the pulse of the tramp's screws beat steadily on my phones.

"Hear anything on sound?" Captain Warder demanded. "Is she increasing speed?"

"No, Captain. No change at all," I reported.

We maneuvered for a second attack. Suddenly the diving alarm sounded. "Clear the bridge! Stand by to dive! Take her down!"

The night lookouts scrambled down the conning tower, the hatch slammed shut, the bolts wheeled into place, and the *Wolf* knifed down into the sea at a terrific angle. I hung onto my seat.

What had gone wrong up there? Had we been strafed by planes? We leveled off. Now I heard the screws of the tramp grow louder. "She's coming in closer, Captain, much clos—"

Captain Warder broke in. "Let's go deep!" he shouted. The *Wolf* plunged down, down ...

The first charge came. It was far to our port side, and the boat shook as if a chill were running down her spine. More followed, fifteen seconds apart. They were still far from the target. Paul took off his earphones and wiggled his finger in his ear.

"Looks like they're arming all those tramps with charges," he said, annoyed. "What the hell won't they think of next!"

Gus Wright ducked into the shack for a minute. He had his apron on, and his hands were white with flour. "Think it's a decoy?" he asked. "Get busy there, boys." He grinned and vanished.

Several more charges went off. From her screws I knew she was zigzagging all over the place. Finally her screws died out.

She had vanished, most probably into Dili Harbor which the Japs were using. What had happened up there? What sent us down so fast? I left Paul on sound and stepped out into the control room to investigate. Gunner Bennett, who had the watch at the Christmas Tree, waved me over.

"Hear what happened?" he asked. "That sure was a close one."

"Close one?" I didn't get it. From the sound gear, she hadn't sounded that dangerous. "What do you mean?" I asked.

"Well," he said, "there we were up, on the bridge, watching this damn tramp, when all of a sudden there's a big flash and something goes singing over my head."

"You mean they were shooting at us?" I asked, astonished.

Gunner rubbed his knee and looked at me. "It wasn't the ship's cook throwing potatoes," he said dryly. "The shrapnel pock-marked the conning tower."

It was the first time Jap bullets ever hit the *Wolf.* When we thought of the *Wolf* being marked up like that—the finest sub in the Navy—we were burned up.

Whatever the case, we had to move fast now. That Jap tramp certainly must have sent out the alarm. The Japs knew we were around here now. Captain Warder pushed on. We were on the offensive now. We reached a point outside the harbor, and maneuvered in close to the beach, taking the utmost care in the mined entrance. The water was shallow. The crew waited tensely.

Captain Warder upped his periscope and gave us a running account.

"See several masts in the harbor—all sailing schooners. Here's the town. White steeple, church ... Wonder if the Dutch are still fighting. Here's the airport. No activity. Seems to be a radio station here—I see the radio tower. I could shell this place at night ... yet the Japs may have shore artillery."

We set a new course. About halfway to our destination, Ensign Mercer, at the periscope, spoke up. "Here's some smoke," he said. "Zero one zero. Down periscope. Tell the Captain we've sighted smoke."

From his stateroom Captain Warder sent word, "Keep your eye on the smoke, Jim."

After two or three five-minute observations, Ensign Mercer upped the periscope again. "Mark the bearing ... He's coming this way. Call the Captain!"

Captain Warder hurried up into the conning tower and took over.

"I can't make out any part of her yet, she's too far away," he said. Then there was a silence for nearly five minutes. "I can make out her mast ... Bearing 008 ... Range 10,000. Set a course to intercept. Down periscope." Three minutes later he stole another look. *"Hmmmm,* this is a beautiful ship," he said slowly. "Looks like one of those silk carriers."

You knew he was eager to get her. I had her screws in my phones.

"Battle stations!" he ordered. "Tell the boys we have a big ship up here all alone, unescorted. At least I don't see any escorts. Sound, pick him up yet?"

"I got him, Captain," I reported. "Sounds like a Diesel job."

"Looks like Diesel, Eckberg," he said. "Modern ship ... four-goal poster. Looks like a fast freighter. Length about 450 feet. Two masts. Raked funnel. Two passenger decks. Number on stack, can't make it out. Speed, about twelve knots. Straight course. Probably bound for Dili. Loaded, probably. Down periscope. Normal approach course."

Before he fired, Captain Warder made sure of everything. His commands were crisp and precise. He was determined to get this ship, and he and Ensign Mercer checked and double checked every figure.

Finally, "Fire!"

His eyes on their wake, Captain Warder followed the progress of the torpedoes through the water. I heard them run to the target.

Suddenly, an angry exclamation: "What the hell is this?"

Captain Warder's voice echoed through the boat. "They missed the target. Dammit to hell, what is wrong? One fish climbed right up her side. What's wrong here? Here she comes heading for us. Let's get out of here!"

We went down. Captain Warder took his favorite seat outside the radio room. The depth charges came. Luckily, they were mild. Captain Warder sat there resting his chin in the palm of one hand, the perspiration dripping from him, impervious to the crash and trembling of the *Wolf* as the charges exploded.

He sent word down for Langford, and Squeaky hurried up, looking miserable. With him came Lieutenant Syverson, equally unhappy.

"When did we service those torpedoes?" Captain Warder asked quietly.

"Only last night, sir," said Langford. Lieutenant Syverson added, "I checked them myself last night, Captain. Those fish were perfect."

"I don't understand it," said the Skipper. "Two perfect attacks, and two complete misses. This must stop."

He rose. He was the picture of dejection as he went forward to his room.

All of us felt the same. The supreme disappointment for a submarine crew is to line up a perfect target, aim the fish correctly, and have them miss—and then be followed by your target, all full of vim and vigor and dropping depth charges all around you.

In the control room half a dozen fellows were sitting around the conning-tower ladder. Nobody said anything for a moment. Squeaky leaned against the ladder and growled.

"Jinx, that's what it is—a damn no-good son-of-a-bitch of a jinx."

No one contradicted him. We weren't too superstitious, but this wasn't funny anymore.

We reversed our course and overhauled the ship. We kept her in position that night. The Skipper was determined to get her.

We surfaced in late afternoon. There was no sleeping now. Every man was alert. We stalked our prey all night. We wanted to attack at dawn. The Skipper upped his periscope at 4 a.m. and studied the sea for a long time.

"Well, now ... I should have expected something like this. That's a blinker light off there on the portside. The alarm's out for us, all right. Down periscope."

At 4:10 a.m., I caught the beat of screws. We were in for it. Every Jap ship within a hundred miles was on the alert for us. And, one ship or ten, at false dawn we attacked.

The *Wolf* practically tiptoed in for this one. Not a sound in the ship as we waited the order to fire. Overhead the Jap was calmly steaming along. Finally the order came:

"Stand by to fire ... Fire!"

I could picture the excitement in the torpedo room. Be jerk, his blue eyes alight, his face flushed, slamming the firing knob, slapping the first torpedo-tube door, and yelling as the fish left the *Wolf*: "Go get him, baby! Head for that bastard's belly."

I caught the whine of the fish as they tore through the water.

Squeaky Langford must be nearly berserk now, screaming, cautioning, everywhere at once: "Watch this ... Take it easy, dammit. Get going, you guys ... Move that son-of-a-bitch, will you!"

If ever a sub wanted to sink an enemy ship, this was it. But nothing helped. The Captain's voice came over the intercom.

"All missed aft." Then, a moment later, "Missed completely. Take her down."

His words silenced the entire ship.

I could sit at sound no longer. "I'm going to grab some coffee, Paul," I told Maley.

In the control room some of the crew were talking to Dishman, who was leaning on the sternplanes control. He looked like a mad bull.

Hershey was telling Dishman: "That's the whole answer to it—that observer. That dodo bird we got on board. Hell, nine torpedoes and not a hit! The *Seawolf* never missed that many in her life!"

There was silence. Zerk said dryly: "What the hell, he didn't push the target away, did he?"

"He wasn't here last time, was he?" demanded Hershey. "No. So what happened? We didn't have any misses. We made a score. This run is different. There's a stranger aboard, and the *Wolf* doesn't like it."

I went through to the galley and drew some coffee. Gus Wright was leaning on a shelf of the tiny alcove, working on the menu for the next day.

"Tough luck," I said.

"Plenty tough," he said. "I don't know why the hell I'm worrying about food. I'm not hungry now."

I swallowed the scalding black coffee and went back to my vigil on sound.

Word from the conning tower the next morning was that we were heading for the north. We moved on. For days we recharged at night and dove at dawn. Then near the Celebes, a message came through:

"Patrol for convoy headed toward position Y."

No use crying over spilled milk now. We raced on and took a patrol position at the northeast entrance of Macassar Straits.

Now we found ourselves in a strange and dangerous company. The area was crowded with sampans, some of them carrying big 20-mm. guns. Every time the Skipper upped his periscope he ran into a group of them. We were under constant strain. A sampan with a radio could easily give away our position to corvettes or planes. We scared hell out of some of them when our long black periscope popped up in front of them. They scattered like a flock of wild ducks and headed for shore. We didn't like that either. It might rouse the Jap command.

At one point the Captain, at the periscope, spoke up: "Here's something coming along ... A converted raider ... Well, well! She has a plane aft. Let's get her."

He maneuvered the *Wolf* like a wizard in an attempt to get into proper firing position. If we sank one ship—just one—it would make new men of us. Once or twice it looked as if we were slipping into position, but dammit, no. She was just too fast, and there wasn't anything in the world that a submarine can do against a fast ship out of position.

It was no use. She disappeared over the horizon.

Slowly we moved north. We poked our nose into every cove and inlet, but they were deserted. Finally one night we entered a narrow, shallow channel and surfaced. Suddenly one of the lookouts sang out: "Object on port bow."

We crash dived. My sound gear picked up the flutter of screws—a destroyer, I thought. Now, thinking over that night, a cold sweat still breaks out on me.

The men sat on their stools; they lay in their bunks waiting. I could trace the enemy's course. He was taking his time, searching every inch of that passage. My heart was in my throat. Both Maley and I had our earphones pressed to our ears.

We really were in a very bad spot. Now the Jap was overhead, his screws beating like a train clattering over a bridge. We knew he was using his sound gear, and that, coupled with the knowledge that we were practically trapped in this shallow, narrow channel, gave us one of the worst moments of our lives. We were afraid. We were damn afraid. We waited. His screws came nearer, then they were above us, right above our heads, thundering like doom—and then the thunder and clatter grew less and less, and he was on his way to parts unknown. Not until hours later, when we were certain he was well on his way south, did we straighten out and head north again.

We surfaced at midnight, cruised slowly, and dove before dawn the next morning.

Captain Warder upped his periscope. He gave a low whistle. "This place is heavy with guns," he said. "Let's see ... yes, batteries over here ... over here ... over here ... Big shore batteries on three sides of us. Well," he said, "I'd hate to be a surface ship right now ... Wait a minute, wait a minute! Here's something. Jap freighter ... He's a little baby ... riding high and dry. Probably empty. He's probably heading for the Indies to pick up loot. We have a nice chop up here. Oh, oh! I can see two men on the bridge. They're looking this way, too. Can they see this little bit of stick I've raised? I'd sure like to catch the fellow who said the Nips can't see well. Those babies have been picking us up right along." Pause. "Oh, well, there she goes. We couldn't have attacked her anyway. Well, let's take a look around this way. We won't go too far in—just far enough to see if there's anything worth our trouble."

We poked around inside the bay entrance. We found nothing. After an hour of almost constant observation, we headed out again and kept going until we reached the spot we wanted.

The place was literally swarming with Jap airplanes, and we dove long before dawn. We had a bad time of it, submerged. The sea was rough, we had trouble with our depth control, and we were constantly afraid that at any moment something might go wrong and we'd pop out on the surface. After darkness came, we surfaced. We began to charge batteries. The Captain was on the bridge with his usual deck crew.

Snyder, on sound, suddenly spoke up. "I've got a set of screws here on the port bow," he said.

I jumped. The alarm went like fire to the bridge. It was pitch black up there. We shouted the word up. Still we didn't dive. I took over sound. There were screws! A destroyer! Why weren't we diving? I was about to shout, "Captain, he's damn close—" when there was a shout from the bridge. The diving alarm jangled.

There was a scramble and rush of feet, bodies virtually tumbling down the ladder, a bang as the conning tower hatch slammed shut, and we crash dived. The air hissed through the ship like something alive. The depth-gauge needle twisted in a frenzy. Our incline was so sharp I had to cling to my desk. We plummeted downward.

The Jap ship came beating over us, dropping her depth charges. We expected her back, but she went on past us. Perhaps she was afraid, too.

Not until everything quieted down and the beat of her screws had faded away did we head out from the beach. Then I turned the sound gear back to Snyder and looked up Franz, who'd been on the bridge. I wanted to find out what had happened up there. Why had we dived so late?

Franz was huddled over a hot cup of coffee in the mess hall. He looked as though he'd been through a battle.

"You can say that again," he said. "We had ourselves one hell of a time up there. Those goddamn seas were as high as your neck, that wind was whistling around your ears, I tell you, it was so damn noisy we didn't get the word fast enough. They were yelling to us from the conning tower about this Jap, but we didn't hear them. There we are minding our own business, and suddenly up comes the Captain and starts really looking. I guess he had the word from below. He couldn't have been up on the bridge more than a minute when, bingo! we find ourselves looking at each other. Jesus Christ, that Jap had got his searchlights trained square on us, and we were pinned there like flies on a wall.

"Well," went on Franz, shaking his head, "we sure scrammed for the hatch. I rode Loaiza's shoulders down. But get this, Eck—the Captain is still up there worrying whether everybody is down O.K. We suddenly see he's alone, and then—did he travel! This Jap had us lit like day, and the old man didn't wait for nothing. He smacked the diving alarm as he came down the hatch. After the boat was down and leveled out, I noticed the Skipper leaning against the control-room ladder and laughing until he almost bawled.

"'It's very funny,' he says. 'Here I am on the bridge, wondering if all hands have made the hatch, when it dawns on me that I'm standing there all alone. I'm standing there like a nitwit in that searchlight. My boys are fast, but even if I am older than most of them, I'd surely have passed them getting to that hatch tonight ...'" Franz chuckled.

"'Lucky I had a clear hatch when I hit it,' the old man says. 'Did I feel like a hero standing up there all alone in the limelight!'"

We remained down. Hours passed. Her screws were gone.

We surfaced carefully and completed our battery charge.

Toward noon the next day Captain Warder sighted a ship well in toward the beach. "This is definitely a patrol vessel," he announced. "About three hundred feet long. Looks like a converted yacht. She has the longest depth-charge racks I have ever seen. They extend from the break of the bridge down to the stern. Looks as if she might be loaded with oil drums. I'm going to plunk her if I can."

Our approach continued with frequent observations. The weather was all against us. The waves were monstrous. We were constantly in fear of broaching. Suddenly Captain Warder, at the periscope, his voice surprised:

"What's this? Down periscope! Secure battle stations. Come to course zero ... zero ... zero. She has a plane working with her. It came so close her pontoons splashed water on the periscope. We'll be having company in a few minutes."

We did. A pattern of depth bombs dropped all around us, but they didn't come too close.

Now, of course, we knew our value here was nullified. We had been detected twice, and the Japs were on the alert.

We headed for a new location and arrived before very long.

It was the hottest area we had ever been in. Jap planes, anti-sub vessels, and corvettes patrolled incessantly, guarding their supply lines. One slip meant death, and we knew it. The next four and a half days were to be the most exhausting and nerve-wracking any of us had ever undergone. We were at battle stations continually. We grabbed sleep when we could. We ate with one ear cocked to hear the alarm. Captain Warder virtually lived in the conning tower. He scanned the sea without rest. At dawn of the third day he reported: "Masts and ships on the horizon."

Then he added: "I'm not going to try to mark all these ships; the traffic is exceptionally heavy ... their air coverage is exceptionally heavy. They have a lot of ships ... going in empty and coming out full ... Those babies coming out are loaded right down to the waterline. Probably bound for Tokyo. They're really making hay while the sun shines. Let's go to work, now. Mark ... three five eight ... leading ship, destroyer ... three ships in line. No estimate on the range. Down periscope." He conferred with Deragon and Mercer. He studied his charts. He upped the periscope and looked again. "I have a new type destroyer here," he said. "Stubby mainmast; two turrets forward; lot of anti-aircraft guns; one turret aft. She's leading three big Maru's. They're probably coming out here to a rendezvous point. Down periscope."

He spoke to Mercer: "Now, Jim, what I want to do is to fire at that destroyer and at the leading Maru. We've got good conditions. The water is a little flat, but I think we can get in."

He called down to me: "Eckberg, is this man using his sound gear?"

I'd heard no pinging. "No, sir," I said.

"They probably think this place is invulnerable to submarines," said Captain Warder.

We maneuvered into position and fired. We waited. Captain Warder's forehead was pressed against the periscope. Just then a terrific *ka-boom!* hit my ears through the phones.

"There's a Jap officer in shorts walking up and down the fo'c'stle," came Captain Warder's voice. "They see the wakes ... He's not walking now! He's galloping for the bridge! There go our fish ... missed her! Hell, they missed her!"

"Captain, there was an explosion," I sang out. This was quite unnecessary because everybody in the ship heard it.

"Yes, she went off just the other side of her." He sounded disgusted. "Water shot up higher than her stacks." He watched. "They're panicky," he said. "The destroyer's picking up speed. He's leaning this way ... Down periscope!" Then: "Take her deep." And then: "Rig for depth charge."

We went down and waited. I sat on my little stool, working the sound gear, earphones on my head. Maley was sitting at my left elbow, as busy as I. I could picture Sousa, walking back and forth throughout the ship, saying, "Now, boys, you all set in here? Goddammit, we missed ... I wonder what was wrong?"

Dishman would be grunting as he maneuvered the bowplanes, wearing his cut-off shorts and sandals, his big hammy arms and chest glistening with sweat. At his right Gunner Bennett, intent on his bowplane wheel, glancing now and then at Holden to see if the latter wanted any change. Holden standing one arm behind his back, his legs astride, biting the nails of his right hand, his head turning from right to left as he watched the depth gauges.

Squeaky Langford sitting down in the forward torpedo room, elbow on knee, chin on hand, worried about why the torpedoes missed, expecting to be bawled out. Be jerk standing, hands on hips, head down, watching the sound shafts to see that nothing went wrong. Gus Wright, walking about in the after-battery room testing valves above his head to see they were tight. Swede Enslin, legs apart, standing at hydraulic manifold, hands on two levers, looking at his Christmas Tree, then at Holden, his head swinging from one to another. At the air manifold, Red Jenkins, holding the big spin bar in his hands, looking at the air gauges, very calm. And, his head through the after-battery hatch, peering into the control room, Doc Loaiza, rubbing his face, muttering: *"Dios, Dios, Dios!"* ...

Lieutenant Deragon would be at the fire-control unit, absolutely absorbed in the picture created before him; he'd probably not even heard "Rig for depth charge," because he'd missed; standing there as if to say, "What went wrong here? It looked perfectly good to me." Captain Warder, directly behind him, leaning against the control-room ladder, deep in thought, his right elbow cradled in his left palm, his right hand fingering his beard, thinking, thinking, thinking hard! ... The mess cooks washing the morning dishes, one man wiping; depth charges coming or no, dishes had to be taken care of. Sully putting on his battle telephones, wondering where his mess boys were, and if they'd closed all valves. Our observer sitting in the Captain's stateroom, reading a magazine, very bored, depth charges or not....

But the depth charges never came.

About 10 a.m. Captain Warder said, "Well, I guess they're not going to give us the rock and roll. Maybe we did hurt him. Maybe he can't depth-charge us. I think I'll go up and take a look."

As he was about to order, "Up periscope," I picked up enemy activity.

"Captain, they're looking for us," I warned.

Captain Warder demanded, "What does he seem to be doing?"

I said, "He's pinging; I can't pick up his screws. He must be quite a ways off."

We came up cautiously. The Skipper took a fast look. "Here's a little launch over here; he's just floating around; that's probably the fellow who's looking for us. My, he's a little thing!"

We started up the hydraulic pump, and the Jap heard us and came toward us like a flash.

"That won't do. Down periscope," snapped the Skipper.

"This fellow seems pretty intent on what he's doing. He probably knows we're around here. Let's take it easy for a while and see if we can't shake him."

That launch was a pest. He had sound equipment, and his sound man was an expert. Maley and I were both astounded by the methodical type of searching he employed. The afternoon wore on. We couldn't shake him. He may not have been equipped to depth-charge us, but he could easily have called his friends, and there were plenty of them around. Six o'clock. Seven o'clock. It was dark upstairs now, but we still dared not surface.

This Jap was too good. We stayed down.

Every little while Captain Warder was at the door of the radio shack. "What do you hear?"

My report was always the same. "Captain, we just aren't shaking this guy."

"Persistent cuss," the Captain said. "Let me know if there's any change."

We stripped our running machinery to a minimum. The only motors kept operating were those necessary to keep the ship maneuverable, and the sound-gear apparatus. Maley and I never underestimated a Jap sound man again.

Finally, about 1 a.m., with our batteries dangerously low, Captain Warder decided we'd surface and if necessary make a run for it. The Jap was now behind us, not too far away. We made ready for anything. Captain Warder was the first man on the bridge, and his eyes must have been glued to his night glasses a second after he hit the bridge. I was worried about aircraft. We were fresh meat for any plane that spotted us. It was a bad spot to be caught in. But we maneuvered and changed course to get rid of him, and finally lost him in the night.

We dove again before dawn and came in from a different angle than before. We wanted to sink Jap shipping, and we wanted it bad. In the first hours of daylight a large convoy passed us. A minute's study, and we knew they knew we were there. They sailed by. Shortly after noon we sighted a large cargo ship, escorted by a bristling Japanese destroyer. It was an easy approach. We fired our fish. One hit with an ear-splitting blast that nearly shook our teeth loose. The destroyer came charging down at us, heaving depth charges right and left, but between the charges I heard the death rattle of the cargo ship over my earphones.

I told the Captain: "She's sunk, Captain. I heard her go."

Everyone cheered. There was no end of back-slapping and congratulations. The morale of the entire ship soared. We'd broken the jinx.

Gus Wright celebrated by producing a platter of Spam sandwiches and mugs of steaming black coffee. But we didn't have much chance to enjoy them. The depth charges came. How they rained them down! They depth-charged to the right, to the left, ahead of us, and behind. The ocean churned with the explosions. We were rocked and shaken, but no damage was done. Maley and I sat through the attack with the phones on. Some of the blasts were so near our ears were paralyzed. We couldn't speak to each other, but at times I would look over at Maley and catch him with a big grin on his face. Both of us were as pleased as hell.

The depth-charging continued intermittently. We steered a straight course out to sea, but the destroyer followed us out part of the way and pounded our tail.

After a while, Captain Warder said over the intercom, "All right, Eck, take a good listen all around."

I made a very careful search, for this was a dangerous place. I knew Captain Warder was preparing to surface the *Wolf*. I listened intently, investigating every little sound, as I covered the dial, a fraction of a degree at a time.

The Captain upped his periscope, looked about, and exclaimed: "Here's something! ... By God, it is a ship!"

"I think he heard us. Down periscope!" said the Captain slowly, deliberating each word. It looked as if we were to undergo another exhausting night session.

Captain Warder was talking it over with Mercer. "Well, they probably know we're here, all right, but that fellow didn't look as though he could give me too much of a fight on the surface. We'll surface and run away from him. The crew's tired, I'm tired, and I want some fresh air in this ship. Stand by to surface."

We held our breath as the *Wolf* climbed to the surface. If we came up within range of the enemy, he would blow us to bits.

We broke the water. "Open the hatch!"

A gust of fresh air swept through the ship. The lookouts rushed to the bridge. We heard the cry: "Ship on the port bow!"

By a miracle we hadn't come up directly alongside of her.

Then, listening intently, I heard the stealthy turning over of her screws. She had seen us.

"She's coming after us, Captain," I warned.

"I can see her, Eckberg," came his unperturbed voice from the bridge, "but she'll never catch us. We have too much of a head start."

We raced through the darkness and lost her.

The next day we again started our penetration. We worked against stiff odds. The Japs knew we were there, and they were employing every device they had to keep us from attacking. We were still out a way when Captain Warder picked up a ship. We raced to battle stations. We were pepped up. "It's a man-of-war," announced the Skipper, and we were really on our toes, then. Captain Warder went after him. We were about 6,000 yards away when he upped periscope for another look. He peered intently for a few seconds, then a loud, explosive "Dammit!" We knew that the target had zigged radically, or something new had entered the picture. We didn't have long to wait, though. We all heard Captain Warder clearly.

"This isn't a destroyer. It's a damned anti-sub ship, something like a corvette. Secure battle stations. Come left to zero eight zero and let's head out of here."

Listening to the Jap, I knew he was not wasting his energies wandering about. His course was straight, and the sudden thought that he might have a plane working with him—a plane that had already spotted us—flashed through my mind. I heard the growl of his screws. They were coming closer, fast and powerful. It was time to warn the Captain.

"He's heading right for us, Captain," I sang out.

The Skipper said, "Are you sure, Eckberg? I don't think he saw our periscope."

I said, "Positive, Captain."

Maley, at my side, nodded agreement.

"I'll have a look around and see what he's doing," said the Skipper.

The sound of the Jap's screws grew more intense. They bored into my brain. He was coming in for the kill. We were no longer the hunter but the hunted. I screamed, "Captain, he's dead astern ... He's coming over us ... He's ready ..."

Captain Warder didn't give me a chance to finish. *"Right full rudder! All ahead full!"*

That last command saved our lives. A second later a thunderclap split my eardrums, and a knifelike pain slashed through my head. The photographs bounced off my arm. Dust from a million hidden crevices clouded the sound shack. Maley flew off his chair and landed with a crash on the deck. I was swept off my stool and landed next to him. Bits of cork mixed with the dust. Our heavy sound gear rocked and swayed.

I kept tearing at my earphones, trying to get them off before another thunderbolt should split my head. From far off I heard Captain Warder's shout, "Take her deep!"

He didn't have to give that command. The depth charge was so close it smashed us down into the sea. It was the closest call the *Wolf* had ever had. Again and again the Jap dropped his charges. Each one rocked the *Wolf*. Every plate, every rivet must have been put in her with a prayer, for somehow they held. Water roared through the superstructure, sounding as if it were traveling a hundred miles an hour. Through my mind flashed, *Now the shack is getting a real cleaning!* I saw Maley fighting to get to his feet. With each charge he slammed against the bulkhead and was forced to his knees like a punch-drunk fighter. He was wearing a pair of faded shorts, and he looked like a man in a ring. Bits of cork stuck to the stubble on his face. He looked dazed. Then he glanced at me, shook his head, and laughed. He couldn't control himself. He was depth-charge happy.

I began to laugh, too. We sat there in the midst of hell, laughing until the tears rolled down our cheeks and we were gasping for breath.

"What are we laughing for?" Maley managed to get out, and, laughing, I tried to say, "We're so goddamn silly-looking, sitting here ..."

Then silence. Painfully I got to my feet and back at the sound gear. I heard the retreating screws, fainter and fainter. Had we scared him away?

Captain Warder plopped down into his chair outside the sound shack. "Where's he now?" he asked. "What's he up to now?"

For the next hour there wasn't a sound in the boat except the Captain's voice asking for bearings. Finally I could report, "He's gone, sir."

Captain Warder rose heavily from his chair. "Good!" he said, and walked slowly away. We never knew why he fled.

"I'm going to hit the sack, Eck," Maley said. I buried my face in my hands and fought to keep awake.

It was many days now since we had tasted fresh air and felt the sun. When I finally got to my own bunk, I was so keyed up I couldn't fall asleep. We were working near a bad mine field. Anti-sub patrol boats were all over the place. We'd never know when we might surface in the night and have a battery of Jap guns blow us out of the water. We were absolutely alone.

We had attacked and attacked—and failed.

I couldn't keep Marjorie out of my mind now. I lay in my bunk and looked up at the photographs. Something told me she needed me. When I did fall asleep, I slept badly.

Call it telepathy or what you want. That night, nearly halfway around the world, Marjorie did need me. She was near death with pneumonia. The physicians had nearly given up hope. They told her mother so. That night Marjorie repeated over and over again: "I must live for Spike. I must live for Spike." And one time, in the early hours of the morning, she sat up in bed and called in a clear, loud voice: "Mel, Mel, come in here! What are you standing out there for? Mother, go over and tell him to come in here!" She stared into the darkness and then lay back and fell asleep.

When we checked the date, it was the same day, almost to the hour, that the Jap ship was dropping the pattern of depth charges that nearly finished the *Wolf*. Marjorie always said she could have sworn I was standing outside her room that morning, staring in at her with a strange, helpless smile.

The next day I felt better. A load seemed lifted from my shoulders. Word came through that we were ending this patrol soon. We'd be heading for Australia again. The crew became light-hearted. Zerk, Eddie Sousa, and Swede came into the control room in the afternoon and began shooting the breeze. Zerk had his pipe under full draft and said he would fight the first man that tried to put it out.

"That damn thing kills a bug at ten feet, Zerk," Swede told him. "Someday it'll kill all of us."

Zerk just looked at him.

Someone brought up the last depth-charge attack.

"It's that jinx, that's what it is," Swede said, pounding his big fist on his knee.

Zerk nodded in a cloud of smoke. "That damn observer we're carrying," he said. "Without him, we'd have knocked off every one of those bastards."

We tuned in on the radio to see what our old friend, Tokyo Rose, had to say. She was in her usual good form. She put an old Rudy Vallee record on this time, and we listened to that. Somewhere she found a Benny Goodman record, and we thought that was a nice touch.

"American submarines have been detected and have been vigorously dealt with by the Imperial Fleet," she announced triumphantly. "Several of the large undersea raiders are known to have been sunk."

We laughed. Out at Christmas Island we'd been a "nest of Allied submarines." We were doing all right, we decided.

The auxiliary crew spent some time now going over the *Wolf* with a fine-tooth comb. Zerk summed up the damage. "Just a couple of pipes sprung a leak," he said. "She's not hurt bad. I understand that one of Gus's Silex coffee-pots was smashed, though."

We all groaned. One less coffeepot was a major calamity.

Gus later broke the news to us that from now on our menu would consist of dehydrated potatoes, rice, and bread. There'd be canned meat, but no butter. What we had left had turned bad. Most of the meat we took on at Australian ports was mutton and Australian hare, both of which were too gamey for us. We were beef and pork eaters, and we didn't like Australian meat. I found that I was eating less than usual. My throat was beginning to hurt. For two or three days at a time, it hurt every time I swallowed. Doc Loaiza fixed up a gargle, but it didn't help much.

The new diet wasn't anything to write home about, bad throat or no bad throat. The potatoes tasted like balls of cotton. The meat was Spam, which is fine if you like it. Most of us lost our appetites. If it hadn't been for Gus Wright's fresh bread, I don't know what we would have done. It was delicious, soft, with a nice even brown crust that melted in your mouth.

Our washing machine was going full blast now with most of the boys getting ready for liberty, pushing each other aside trying to monopolize the mirror in the washroom. Sousa battled with the black gang in the engine room about messing Baby up with their oil-drenched clothes.

"All they do," he complained to me, "is throw their stuff in the machine and don't give a damn how she looks when they leave her. I'll knock the bastards' heads off if I catch them."

Swede was the only man who refused to use Baby. "The hell with her," he said. "I'll never wash my own clothes. It ain't American."

It was a nightly joke to see Swede pull out his "locker stick"—a long piece of wood used to pick soiled clothes out of a locker—and look through soiled shorts, shirts, and dungarees for a clean change. His locker was bursting, and yet he'd invariably dig out a new pair of shorts or a clean shirt.

"What did I tell you?" he'd chuckle. "Always one more."

Captain Warder read and relaxed in his room. His desk was piled high with magazines and best sellers. Behind the green monk's-cloth curtain his little stateroom was a model of neatness and efficiency, with a picture of his family—his wife and four youngsters—on the desk, his logs and papers neatly piled in place. He was finishing Van Loon's *Geography,* reading the *Naval Institute Proceedings*, a navy magazine popular among officers, and *The Army and Navy Register*. He also had a copy of *Wuthering Heights* in his room. At night he'd join his officers—Deragon, Mercer, Syverson, and Holden—in a game of hearts in the wardroom. We always knew when he slipped the queen to one of his men. His booming, ringing laugh—he laughed infrequently, but it was loud and contagious when he did—would fill the tiny wardroom and echo in the passageway.

This routine, easy, without strain, went on for a week. We were sticking our nose into every cove, and inlet, and bay. The Captain was still ship-hungry. He wanted to come back with something. We'd just had too much bad luck so far.

On the fifth day we were proceeding submerged when the conning-tower officer spotted a patch of smoke. He called the Skipper, and both agreed it would be a race between the *Wolf* and darkness if we wanted to plunk her. Captain Warder had to be very cautious now. We were near the lower Philippines and had to watch for possible aircraft attack. He upped periscope now and then. Once he said:

"Damn it, there's two of them. They're both coal-burning tramps, merchantmen, high masts, high stacks, probably jumping from one island to another. They are not zigzagging. Both are old Marus ... Battle stations!"

After a pause: "We'll fire from the forward tubes. It's getting dark here. Can you hear them yet?"

I searched. "Not yet, Captain."

The approach party set to work. I had the heartbeat of the Jap screws. They were coal-burners, all right. Maley joined me. We wanted one of these babies badly. I began to call out bearings.

"Make ready the forward tubes," came the Skipper's voice. "Open the outer doors. Willie, I don't know if I can fire on these or not, it's so dark up here now. Has sound got them?"

Lieutenant Deragon said, "Bearings coming along satisfactory, sir."

"Okay, Willie," said the Skipper. "Take her from here."

The Jap was close now. He was lumbering along at ten knots or so. It was only a matter of seconds before Lieutenant Deragon snapped:

"Fire one!"

Immediately we caught the high whine of the fish traveling hot and straight. I looked at my stopwatch to time them. I saw the seconds ticking away. Maley and I watched the fine thin hand slowly crawl around the face of the watch.

Captain Warder climbed down from the conning tower. He passed the sound room. One glance at his face, and we knew that, bad as we felt, he must feel worse.

"I'm going back to see Deragon, Paul," I said. I found him sitting in the control room, toying with a pencil in his shirt and looking miserable.

"Were our bearings correct, Lieutenant?" I asked.

"You men were correct, Eck," he said wearily. "We checked your bearings. I don't know what could have gone wrong."

I felt a little better. At least sound hadn't been at fault.

That night the crew talked about the jinx. They had joked about it before, but now they didn't know what to believe. Before I hit the sack I turned on the radio and heard that the *Swordfish* had taken a large toll of tankers and transports.

Three days out of port, I went topside. It was the first time for many days and nights. I climbed out on deck. The glare was blinding. It was like staring into a brilliant searchlight. I should have known better from my last experience, but I wanted to be up there. I buried my face in my hands. Pain stabbed at my eyeballs. I held onto the rail. I gulped the fresh air. For the first time I knew how exhausted I was.

Late that day I went up again. This time the glare wasn't so bad. My eyes were becoming used to it. When the other men came up, I realized that the crew of the *Wolf* looked like men in a nightmare. These long patrols didn't do us any good. Our faces were gray. Our lips were so dry that a few days later a plague of fever sores broke out among us. Our faces peeled. As before, ordinary daylight sunburned us.

Captain Warder, who had temporarily halted his setting-up exercises, was up on deck now, starting them all over again. I took a look at the bridge. The *Wolf* was as bedraggled as her crew. A blanket of slimy moss covered the deck. The chains were rusted and looked as though they hadn't been used in years. The hawsers were soggy. They lay curled and decomposing under the deck. Where paint had chipped off, leaving the dull steel bare, the *Wolf* looked like a mangy dog. There were signs of where the garbage gang had tossed their nightly swill overboard. There were several places where the acid contents of the stuff had etched into the paint.

At one spot the aft portside was stove in—testimony to our nearly fatal depth charge. The memory of that moment was still vivid in my mind. Again I heard the awful thunderclap that seemed to tear my head apart; again I choked and gagged with the dust and cork.

As port grew closer, we went over the *Wolf* with cloth and polish. We wanted to bring her in spick and span. Magically she began to gleam again, though she still bore her scars. It would take more than polish to hide that wound in her side.

At the entrance to the mine field outside the Australian port, we were met by the U.S.S. *Isabel*. She brought us in alongside a tanker, and we fueled up. Mail came aboard, and for the next few minutes there wasn't a sound throughout the boat.

Marjorie's letters, answering those I'd written the last time I was here, awaited me. Everything was all right. She and Spike were O.K. She'd had pneumonia, she said, but she was all over it now. Not until later, much later, did I learn of the strange coincidence—the strange awareness we both had of each other that night she nearly died.

The following morning we were all called together, and the Skipper made a little speech.

"I don't want any of you to feel that you have neglected your jobs or that you have let me down in any way on this patrol," he said. "We made a tough cruise, and we had our share of tough luck. But don't let that get you down. Remember, you're the crew of the *Seawolf*. You can hold up your heads with anyone. I hope to be with you when we set out to sea again."

We looked at each other. Was Captain Warder leaving us?

That, it appears, was his first inkling that he would soon be given another command—perhaps a more important command—in the future.

He continued: "And I want to say, 'Well done and congratulations.' Now go ashore and have a good time. That's what I'm going to do."

He turned to Lieutenant Deragon. "Anything else, Willie?"

Lieutenant Deragon cautioned us about talking ashore. And that was all.

We worried a little about what Captain Warder's future plans were. Swede said it for all of us. "This is the way I feel about it. I hate like hell shipping out if we lose Freddy." We had come to depend on him so much we couldn't bear the thought of shipping out to sea under a new skipper.

The first night in port I met an old friend, Chief Torpedoman Francis Morales. He was having a beer with Sousa in Sousa's room. The last time I'd seen Morales he was a husky man, pushing a big paunch in front of him. Now he looked almost haggard. He must have lost forty pounds. His hands shook when he lit a cigarette. He had been on the Rock, he said, almost to the end.

The Japs, he said, were devilishly clever. They worked on you every which way. "They wear you down physically," he said, "and then they start on your minds. Before the end, those sons-of-bitches set up big loud-speakers on the Mariveles side of the shore, and they'd play American records at us—one song over and over again."

"What records?" I said.

"They played 'I'm Waiting for Ships That Never Come In,'" he said. "Then they'd play a weepy Christmas song sung by Bing Crosby. It would break your heart. Over and over again, blaring out over the water, like that. I tell you, it was horrible there at night. The boys were half-starved, they were sick and shaking with malaria, the wounded were crowding the Rock's tunnels, and those bastards were playing Christmas songs."

Months later I learned Morales' true story. He was one of the most daring men on the Rock. He'd learn the location of Jap military stores, beg half a dozen sticks of dynamite, wrap them in waterproof paper, and get a PT boat to take him out to sea. Then, the dynamite tied to him, he would swim through the shark-infested waters to the beach, sneak through the Jap guards, plant the dynamite, set the fuse, and sneak back to the boat. He did this many times. After that he volunteered to sneak through the jungle to gather information on Jap positions. He never got caught. He was a good and a brave man.

That first night, when I got back, I had troubles of my own. My throat began to pain terribly. The next day it was worse. The pain was intense when I swallowed. I went to the doctor on the tender. He looked me over.

"You've got bad tonsils, chief," he said. "Very bad. It's the hospital for you."

At the hospital I was told they'd have to take them out.

CHAPTER IX

Anchored in Sick Bay

I WAS told I'd be operated on in an Australian hospital. It was crowded with patients at the time and, since I was only a minor case, I waited. The *Wolf* remained in port several weeks and sailed on another mission more than a week before I went on the operating table. When I knew she was gone, I felt lower than I'd been in weeks. I don't think I realized until then how much that steel hulk and the officers and men inside her meant to me. I saw pictures in my mind of the *Wolf* cruising along on the surface. I could hear the order, "Clear the bridge!" I saw the Skipper maneuvering for the kill. I knew then that nothing the Japs could do, save sending us to the bottom, could be as bad as being on the beach while my own ship was out to sea.

I was finally admitted to the hospital. It was a magnificent modern institution, the acme of medical efficiency. After I'd been divested of my clothes, had taken a shower, and put on a pair of roomy pajamas, I was given a bed. I was ready to drop off to sleep when a nurse came in with tray and a hypodermic.

"What's that for?" I asked, a little alarmed.

"You're due at the operating theater in about an hour and a half. We're just getting you ready," she said.

"Fine," I said. "Let's get it over with."

She bent over me, swabbed my left arm, and stuck the hypo in.

"Now you just take it easy," she said.

I looked at her. "What was that shot you gave me?" I asked.

"Why, that's morphine, to relax you," she said.

Uh, oh, I thought. I'd had previous experience with morphine. I knew how I reacted to it. It might relax other people. It knocked me out for hours.

"Did you say they wanted me up there in about an hour and a half?" I asked.

"Yes," she said. "Why?"

"Well, miss," I said, "I hope that was a weak shot of morphine you gave me. Just wait and see," I said. I lay there, and it was just as I expected. My feet fell asleep. Then my hands and arms became numb. Just about this time two of the largest men I've ever seen in my life came to my bunk and without as much as a "How do you do?" picked me up as though I were a child, set me into a wheel chair, and started wheeling me away. I felt as though I were floating. I don't remember arriving at the "theater." It seems the operating room was in use when the two Aussies brought me there, so they left me outside the door. That's the last I remember.

I was told later that the doctor who was going to assist the surgeon came out, looked at me, shook me, got no result, called for the surgeon. He took a good look at me and sent for the two giant orderlies to come and get me. They wheeled me back to my bunk and dumped me there. I woke up twelve hours later. I didn't know what time it was, but it was dark. I thought, *Well, that wasn't bad. I didn't even feel them take out my tonsils. These Aussie medics are O.K.* I knew that after a tonsillectomy your throat feels sore, so I took a chance and swallowed. My throat felt swell. I attributed this to the fact that I was so rugged. I even smoked a cigarette, and it tasted fine.

I was lying there comfortably, congratulating myself, when a night nurse came by.

"How do you feel?" she asked.

"Fine," I said, grinning at her. "There was nothing to it."

"No," she said, "that's right. There wasn't anything to it." I thought I detected a sarcastic note in her voice, but I overlooked it because I felt so good.

"When can I leave here?" I asked. "I feel swell. No use staying any longer than I have to."

"Well, I don't know," she said. "That all depends on when they take your tonsils out."

"When they— What!" I must have shouted it, because heads started popping up all around the ward.

"I said," she repeated quietly, "when they take your tonsils out. You blacked out yesterday morning. Why didn't you let us know you were allergic to morphine?"

I was angry. "Why didn't you let me know you were going to use morphine?" I demanded. "How do I know what you're going to use in a place like this? For all I know it might be anything from dog blood to brain juice you're sticking into me!"

"Well," she said coldly, "there's no doubt that you've had both those injections. Now, will you please be quiet?" And she walked away.

I was burning mad. I got up and sneaked into the kitchen and robbed the refrigerator of two pounds of assorted foods. I gulped them down. Then, smug and self-satisfied, I got back into bed.

The next morning about 10 o'clock a Dr. Smith came around. He was young and pleasant.

"Well, chief," he said, "how do you feel?"

"Fine," I said. "When are we going to get this over with?"

"Oh, let's see," he said. "Today's Tuesday. Let's make it tomorrow morning, shall we?"

"The sooner the better, as far as I'm concerned," I said. "I've already had them out once—or so I thought."

"Yes," he said, smiling. "I heard about it from the head nurse. What did you do? She's all up in the air about the way you talked to one of her nurses."

"Listen, doctor," I said. "I came out number two in that conversation and there were only two of us here. You don't have to worry about any repetition."

"All right, chief," he said. "I didn't pay too much attention to it. Not many of the people here realize that you submarine men hate hospitals."

"Well, I'm afraid I blew up, but I thought you'd taken my tonsils and I had just finished complimenting myself on how tough a guy I was."

Dr. Smith burst out laughing. "Well, chief," he said, still laughing, "you might have to be pretty tough at that, seeing as how we can't dope you."

With that, he walked off. I didn't feel too good the rest of the day, and all the nurses and fellow patients had satisfied smirks on their faces. I read a bit—there were magazines about—and waited. There wasn't anything else I could do. The next morning I woke up, took another shower, and was sitting on my bunk when word was passed for me to "proceed to the theater."

"What?" I exclaimed. "No escorts? No wheelchair?" They didn't think I needed it, they said. That was all right with me. I got up and walked out of the ward, sweating a little, and made my way up to the theater. As luck had it, I met a wheelchair coming back. There was a patient in it. He looked pretty bloody.

"What happened to him?" I asked the orderly wheeling him.

"Oh, nothing," he said. "Just had 'is bloomin' tonsils out."

A little shaky, I walked into the theater, and there was Doctor Smith.

"Good morning, chief," he said cheerily. "Are you all set? Here, sit down."

I sat down.

"Now, Eckberg," he said, "let me talk to you. You see this big needle? Well, I'm going to put cocaine in and around your tonsils. Then we're going to wait until you hit the drooling stage before we go to work. Now, these needles are going to hurt more than the actual cutting. I want to tell you that."

I nodded.

"Now, if you're ready, here's what I want you to do. I'm going to sit on this chair directly in front of you. You put your knees inside of mine. Now, when these needles go in, if you feel like fighting them, grab my legs here." He indicated a point just above his knees. "Grab them and hang on. Are you ready?"

"Let 'er fly, doc," I quavered.

I opened my mouth and grabbed his legs. He was right. The needles did hurt. I did hang on. It was over in a couple of minutes, though.

"O.K., chief," he said. "You did fine on that. You really are tough. Now, just try and relax until that cocaine starts working."

I sat back. I was thinking, *Hell, here I've faced death so many times that just thinking about it becomes monotonous, and here I am quaking at a minor operation. What's the matter with me? The crew would be ashamed of me if they could see me this way now.* Dr. Smith broke into my thoughts by putting something in my mouth that looked like a cross between a check bit for a horse and a muzzle for a mad dog.

"All right," he was saying. "You're drooling. Let's have at them now."

116

All I could do was nod. My tongue was numb. We went into our act again. It couldn't have taken more than ninety seconds this time. But it was a long minute and a half. It didn't hurt so much, but what scared me was a long suction hose they had leading from my mouth into a glass jar. I started bleeding. My blood rushed into the jar. As it rose, I became panicky. I didn't know they had water going in too, to create suction. God, I thought, I'm bleeding to death. I'd heard of grown men bleeding to death in tonsillectomies. I was ready to faint when Dr. Smith pulled off this oral hobble and he was finished, looking at his excavation with a bit of pride. He called another surgeon in, and he complimented him on a neat job. Dr. Smith seemed to remember me then and said:

"Okay, chief. All finished. You can go now. You can expect a very sore throat for a couple of days or so. If you want anything, just yell."

Yell? I couldn't even talk. Then I noticed he was grinning. I grinned back. I gave him a wave and shoved off. My "escorts" of battleship size were waiting outside, and they picked me up and dropped me into a wheelchair, and we headed back for the ward, sweeping people and obstacles out of our way as if they didn't exist, one ahead clearing the path, the other pushing the chair. Then I was in bed.

I lolled on one side and drooled all over a rubber mat provided for that purpose and reflected on my sins. I fell asleep after a little while and must have slept quite some time. When I woke up, I was hungry and my throat was so sore I could have yelled—if it hadn't been for my throat. It was night. A nurse brought a big glass of cold milk to me.

I got a good part of it down. I was still hungry, but she refused to give me anything else. I went to sleep again and slept like a log until I was rudely awakened about five in the morning by two nurses.

I looked inquiringly up at them.

"We're here to bathe you," one said. They were pretty rugged looking nurses. Both must have weighed 180 or better, and both were definitely not the romantic type.

"Give me a what?" I squeaked.

"A bath," one said. "You must have a bath, you know. Now, lay down there like a good one, and this'll be over in a moment."

"Now, just a minute," I said. "It may be true that I need a bath, but if so, I'll do the bathing myself. I don't want any women bathing me."

The biggest one turned to her fellow conspirator and with a nod said, "I don't know why, Violet, all these Americans are alike. They don't want us to bathe them." She turned back to me.

"Why not, young man? I was bathing patients when you were born."

"That may be, madam," I said. "And you might be bathing them after I've gone. But you're not bathing me."

"Oh, come now. Don't be difficult. There's nothing to it, and you'll feel ever so much more comfortable," she said.

I shook my head and prepared to repel boarders.

Without another word the bigger one said: "Stay 'ere with 'im, Violet. I'll fetch 'arold."

Violet and I eyed each other for about five minutes when the other nurse came back with 'arold. And 'arold was one of the two giants who pushed me around in the wheelchair.

"Now, matey," he said, "wot's the trouble 'ere, hey? Look, now lay down there, young man, and let these two ladies bathe you, or I'll have to."

I went to sleep after being thoroughly bathed.

I recuperated in the normal period of time and in the normal way. When I was released, I was homesick. I missed my own home, I missed the *Wolf.* They told me I could have some recuperation leave. I decided I would go to a small town not far away. This was a perfect little town. The food was good, the people friendly, the air marvelous. At the end of the leave I reported back to the submarine tender stationed at the port and was given temporary duty on one of the relief crews—crews that take over a submarine when she comes in from battle and get her ready to go to sea again, when the regular crew rests up.

I was kept busy. One day a rumor spread that the *Wolf* was reported missing. That was one of the worst days of my life. I dropped everything I was doing and rushed up to the Flag Office, in port, headquarters of the operating staff. I was panicky. I could learn nothing. No news was given out, particularly no news about submarines, and though I was a submarine man and identified, I could get nowhere. When liberty started, I went to the nearest pub and tried to forget all about it.

About 4 a.m. the next morning another submarine man put me in a cab, took me back to the tender, and rolled me in my bunk.

When I woke, I still had no news.

Then, one morning, news did come. The *Seawolf* was coming in. She was O.K. I remember I had a handful of tools when I got the word. I turned and ran for the dock, tools in hand, and then I saw the black shape of the *Wolf* coming in. I'd recognize her in a thousand, and, seeing her, I knew that never again in my life would I be as happy as I was in those few dragging minutes as the *Wolf* decreased distance, and slowly came into full, clear focus from the beach. I looked at her, and then I dashed madly up to the Flag Office and asked a yeoman for my transfer papers.

"What transfer papers?" the yeoman wanted to know.

"My orders to go back to the *Wolf*," I said.

He shook his head. "I don't know about that, Eckberg," he said. "I heard some talk a while ago that you were headed for the *Skipjack.*"

I stared at him. Go to another ship? I had been waiting all this time for the *Wolf*, I didn't want any part of the *Skipjack* or any other boat. I wanted the *Wolf.* I wanted home. I tore out of the Flag Office and headed for the gangway. I was going to find my captain and tell him my story.

One of the first persons I saw was Captain Warder walking with several other officers up the dock. I disregarded naval etiquette, traditions, and everything else and rushed up to him.

"What's the matter, Eckberg?" he greeted me. "You look upset."

"I am upset, Captain," I said. "They're going to transfer me to the *Skipjack*."

"Well." He looked at me. "Well?"

"Well, hell, Captain," I said. "I've been waiting for the *Wolf,* and it seems unfair that I go on another boat now."

"So you really want to come home, eh, Eckberg?" he said with a smile. "Well, move your clothes aboard and forget about it." With that he nodded pleasantly to me and walked on.

Did I want to come home? I could have thrown my arms around him.

"Yes, sir, Captain. Thank you, sir," I said. And I was off for the *Wolf* like an Indian runner.

It was good climbing down the conning-tower ladder, into the control room, smelling the familiar odor of warm oil, digging through the boat and seeing all the boys again. It was Sully who finally corralled me and told me about the mission of the *Wolf.*

Evidently it was an easy one.

"You sure missed out on a good one," he said. "We went through a couple of practice runs when we left port, and the old man took her up the coast heading north. We had a rendezvous there, topped off the fuel tanks, and headed for sea.

"We stayed around a patrol area for two days, and just as we were about to leave the second day the old man spotted a ship. Everything was in our favor," said Sully. "We let loose at her. Damned if we didn't miss.

"Well, the Skipper was gloomy as hell all that day. We headed for our next spot on the other side. We were halfway over, and the periscope officer spotted another ship. We went to battle stations. The old man let go another fish. There wasn't any doubt about what we did to that dude—we blew him sky high. I didn't hear any classification on him, but from the way the fellows were talking it must have been a tanker carrying high octane or an ammunition ship loaded down with powder. There wasn't a trace left. The old man looked all over the place. Couldn't find anything. No survivors, no debris, nothing at all.

"That was a real tonic for us. The old man was as chipper as anything after that hisser went up. Nothing much happened the next two days. We were hanging around when all of a sudden, there she is—another target. The old man went in on one of the best approaches he ever made. He maneuvered in to where a miss would have been impossible. The target didn't know we were anywhere around. The Skipper let go and hit her. We didn't sink her, though." Sully paused. "Eck," he said, "this is where you really missed out. This was the first chance since the war began that we really could look over something we'd put a fish into. I don't remember the name of the ship, but I know she belonged to the

English before the war. I think she was listed as a passenger freighter. Not very big, but clean and pretty.

"Well, d'you know what the Skipper did after he sent that fish into her? We drew up to within 300 feet of her, still at periscope depth. The Captain wanted to find out how deep that Nip was in the water. He was going to shoot another fish into her. But, when we get that close, he sees they were abandoning ship.

"So"—Sully grinned—"what do we do but surface!"

"Surface?" I demanded.

"Right. That Nip had no escorts. We surfaced, and I ran up on the bridge and saw Japs hanging onto rafts, boats, and life-belts. We got next to them, all of us trying to find the name of the ship. We finally got it, but not from them. Hell, Eck, you should have seen Sousa. The Captain wanted a life-ring that was floating around, and old Sousa leaped madly over the side, right into the water, and got it. He lost out because there wasn't any name on it.

"Then one of the Nips grabbed our propeller guard and tried to get aboard. He was halfway up, yelling in Japanese. I guess he was trying to pull the *I'm-dying-but-you're-going-with-me act*. Deragon ran down aft and pushed him back. The Jap made several lunges trying to drag Willie in, but Willie was too quick.

"Sousa kept yelling, 'Speak English?' but the Japs wouldn't answer. We must have circled that ship for hours, watching her go down.

"Then we moved up to the Philippines. We patrolled there for about a while, but didn't see a single ship. Then we headed back here."

Sully stopped. He sat back and ran his hands through his hair.

"Now tell me what happened to you," he said. "Get those tonsils out?"

I told him.

CHAPTER X

Tons of Jap Shipping

WE LEFT port soon afterward at 6 p.m. It felt good to shed that shoreside feeling. I'd had enough of land, streets, and people. My throat felt perfect. I wanted to get back into action. We all wanted action. And on this mission we were prepared to prove anything we claimed, too. Lieutenant Mercer had been experimenting taking photographs through the periscope with a 35-mm. camera and fixed it so that he could clip it to the eyepiece and in the conning tower snap a shot of anything we hit.

The first day out we found a notice posted on the bulletin board:

NOTICE TO ALL HANDS:
In case of capture by the enemy, under international law you are required to give the following information: (1) your name, (2) your service number, (3) your rating, (4) your home address. That is all. In case the Seawolf, through enemy action, is damaged to such an extent that you are captured, remember this—we are operating from an advance base, whose name is unknown to any member of the crew, and we are en route to Japan. Under no conditions are you to let any information out.

Well, that was clear enough.

We spent three or four days going up the Australian west coast. We made training dives, fired a few practice rounds of service ammunition, checked our gear, and readied the ship for action. Finally we reached our advance base and fueled to capacity. Then we headed north, entered our old picnic grounds, and headed right up for our first stopping point.

Our first days were uneventful, but the crew was on constant alert. These were some of the most dangerous waters in the Pacific. The sea bottom was treacherous, a crazy quilt of boulders, shoals, and menacing coral reefs. Some of it had never been charted. The fear of striking a reef was on my mind day and night. Maley and I stood an intense sound watch, each of us doing with less than six hours' sleep out of the twenty-four.

On the third day, as we were patrolling, Lieutenant Syverson, conning officer at the time, picked up a target. The call went down for Captain Warder, and the Skipper took over.

The intercom chattered: "She has a two-stick mast ... high bridge ... single-stacker... Range, about 8,000. Looks like a converted passenger liner... She's certainly traveling ... Probably headed for Balikpapan."

This made her a doubly valuable target. We knew from information given us that the Dutch had virtually destroyed Balikpapan, on the southwest coast of Borneo, fabulous for the rich-ness and quantity of its oil. But we knew, too, that the Japs were trying desperately to put the wells back into condition. It was up to us to stop this Jap from getting to Borneo.

I picked up the target. Her course was normal. The order came to fire. We fired.

Seconds ticked by ... a minute now. No explosion yet.

"I can see both of them," said Captain Warder's voice. "They're missing ahead. Now she's seen them ... Here she is, boys ... coming right for us ... Looks scared as hell, too ... Take 'er down ... Rig for depth charge."

While I kept singing bearings out to him, I was wondering what in the hell had happened. Just what was wrong? We waited, silent. But the ship never dropped a charge.

"She's running away," I called out.

The Skipper upped the periscope. "Damn!" he said. "There the bastard goes, heading right back to the barn. He knows damn well I can't follow him. Secure battle stations. Secure depth-charge stations."

Now things were quiet. Had we picked up a new jinx? There was nothing to do but lump it. I wandered into Kelly's Pool Hall and found Eddie Sousa. He felt like cribbage. We sat down and started to play and we hadn't been playing more than ten minutes when we heard the distant, muffled thump of a depth charge. I started to get up, but Sousa said, "Oh, hell. They're a long way off. Let's finish the game."

We finished it and started a second. When a second charge went off Sousa fanned out his cards and said, "Probably sent out a plane to heckle us."

I said: "Could be, Eddie, but I better get back up with Paul."

Sousa began shouting: "Damn you, Eckberg, you know I'm ready to skunk you." He looked so hurt and indignant I couldn't help laughing at him.

He chased me out of the room, yelling: "Come on back here, you yellow dog, and finish this game and get skunked!"

Paul, who'd heard some of it, grinned when I came in. "Someday Sousa will handcuff you to a chair and make you finish that game," he said.

After hearing the charges hit the water, I decided Sousa was right. An air-plane had spotted us, dropped a few aerial bombs, and disappeared.

Sousa came in the sound shack and began to complain bitterly to Maley how I walked out on his winning game. Every time he would begin, I would raise my hand and say: *"Shhhhhhh*, I hear something." This drove Eddie into a frenzy. He wrung his hands and called me every name under the sun. For days afterward he alternately threatened and cajoled me to finish that game. We still have to finish it.

Sometime during the night we heard over the radio the Nazis had been stopped cold in Russia, and that the Marines were pushing the Japs back on

Guadalcanal. Over the radio came word that several of our submarines were working out there in the Solomon Islands invasion.

Maley commented on this. "I'm glad we're not Marines," he said. "Think of crawling on your belly in the jungle waiting for a Jap to take a shot at you. What a life!"

As we were about to surface that night, Captain Warder spotted a large sampan. He told Lieutenant Deragon: "I think I'll look this fellow over. He may be a Nip with a radio transmitter and receiver. If he is, we'll shoot him up."

We surfaced silently and crept up on him. We had not been on the surface over five minutes before Gunner Bennett was down in the control room opening the gun locker and breaking out small arms and some machine guns. We were not going in close without being set for a surprise. Everybody wanted to get a chance to shoot some Japs, but the men who were to do that shooting, if it came to that, were already at their stations.

The Captain maneuvered carefully. No talking was permitted on the bridge. We used our motors. There wasn't a sound of any kind. The Captain kept his glasses on the sampan constantly. We were taking no chances, and the ship was in a crash-dive condition.

I don't believe the sampan knew we were about until we were less than thirty yards from her. The Captain looked the sampan over, bow to stern and back, looking for telltale antennae, any signs of gun mounts—there was nothing. After a few minutes, he said: "It's harmless. The only ones on board are a man, his wife, and two small children."

Gunner Bennett collected the guns. We were all disappointed. We wanted a crack at the Japs at close hand.

We charged batteries and dove shortly before dawn and headed for another enemy port. Twelve hours later we reached our patrol point outside the harbor. In seizing this port, the Japs won one of the most valuable prizes of the war.

Before the Dutch moved on, they put the torch to the entire city. Refineries, cracking plants, millions of dollars' worth of re-search laboratories went up in acrid smoke. Most of the foreign population had fled to Java, or vanished into the jungle. Somewhere in that jungle the Allies had a secret airport of which they made excellent use against Jap shipping in the early part of the war.

Even the workers battled the Japanese invaders. We learned later that employees dumped thousands of barrels of oil into the river to stop the Japs, setting fire to it, but a sudden cloudburst put out the flames.

The Japs were using the harbor for all it was worth, running oil up to the homeland in anything that would float. Three hundred miles up the coast they had seized Tarakan, too, but only after the Dutch had destroyed the oil refineries, which used to produce nearly one million tons a year.

Our first day on patrol was quiet. We cruised in deep water.

But at dawn of the second day the Skipper decided to go inside the harbor. It was a ticklish business, for the Japs had mined it, and we knew the water wasn't too deep. We couldn't afford to make a mistake.

We went in. We went deeper and deeper. The water grew dangerously shallow. The Skipper had his eye glued to the periscope, scanning the beach installations.

"Battle stations!" he ordered suddenly. "Make ready the forward tubes."

The entire boat churned into action. The control party scrambled up the ladder.

"It's a sub chaser." Captain Warder's words were measured.

"I don't know if he saw us. I won't attack unless he does. He's small and making high speed."

This was plenty bad. We were in shallow water. We had nowhere to hide. If he attacked, he could blast us to bits. If he knew we were there, he would attack. It was as simple as that. I listened to the screws, and the thumping of my heart was so loud and strong it seemed to shake me from head to toe. The Japs' screws were faint, then louder, then still louder. Maley pressed his phones against his ears. There wasn't a whisper in the boat. I scarcely recognized my own voice as I gave the bearings: "Three two zero ... three two two ... three two four."

All sorts of things flew through my mind. I was convinced the Jap would pass close to us, but the pattern of his bearings indicated that he would pass well forward on our bow unless he changed his course radically. But in the back of my mind I knew a plane might have been working with the subchaser, must have spotted us, and put the subchaser on our tail. I found my fist beating the desk in time with the beating screws. Louder ... louder ... up the bow—up the bow— and past us, a good 600 yards away, at high speed.

Captain Warder sat back on his stool and looked about. "That was a close one," he said with a grim smile. "I guess he's going out to meet someone."

We began to dive again. We waited and listened, and then went into deeper water. We surfaced at dusk and dove as usual at dawn, to re-enter the harbor. Shallow water or not, mines or no mines, we still had work to do. I heard surf breaking on the beach, the water crashing and clashing over shoals and reefs. But the Skipper brought the *Wolf* into that harbor as daintily as a ballet dancer.

All through the morning and into the afternoon we inched our way forward, gathering information. Lieutenant Holden was at the periscope and began to describe what he saw.

"I see a lot of houses over there," he said. "Now I see trees ... there's a big clump. Now what's this? Looks like a radio antenna." Pause. "Battle stations! ... Call the Captain! ... Left rudder, Rudy! All ahead full!"

The *Wolf* leaped forward. We were in shallow water. This was doubly dangerous. Something was up. Holden's voice:

"I was busy scanning, Captain, and I took a look behind us; and there, almost on our port beam, is a big tanker and an escort. I think we can get them."

The Skipper took over the periscope. He whistled.

"She certainly is a big one ... Too bad she didn't come in before ... That's our friend of yesterday coming in with her. O.K.," he said. "Down periscope. We'll try and get in." We plowed at full speed into even shallower water. Then we cut our speed, and Captain Warder upped his periscope. "Damn it, she's drawing away from us," he said. "Nothing we can do. Secure battle stations. We'll trail her in and see if we can get a shot."

We followed that ship right into the mouth of a fresh-water river. The Captain tried every trick he knew stalking her, but she was too far ahead of us.

Captain Warder would have preferred to wait outside the harbor and catch the tanker, but our schedule called for a change. Reluctantly we gave up the hunt and continued up the coast.

On the way the conning officer picked up a smudge of black smoke. It looked like a fat freighter. We went through several maneuvers, were annoyed by a series of brief rain squalls, and finally, about five hours later, we caught up with our target. It turned out to be a seagoing tug!

We were several days without sighting anything of importance. At times the Skipper, who was getting ship hungry, took the *Wolf* so close to shore we would have been able to swim in. The night of the fourth day, Lieutenant Deragon, dropping in to chat, told me where we were heading.

"And from there?" I asked. He smiled noncommittally. I knew we would learn soon enough. Next day the word had gotten around to the crew, and all kinds of rumors flew about. First we were going to Brisbane, then Pearl Harbor, then Dutch Harbor, and finally Midway. Something told me we were on our way home. It was now many months since we had left Cavite. We had already been out a long time on this patrol.

Home seemed so far away that night. How would my son greet me? I put my hands behind my head and looked up at their photographs—Marjorie and Spike. Well, they'd waited a long, long time. For months now, in our letters, we had been planning what our first night would be like. We'd settled on dinner in some quiet little restaurant, candles on the table, a full-course meal, topped off by a bottle of expensive wine that had to rest in a bucket of ice. We wouldn't discuss the war. Marjorie wouldn't talk to me about the *Wolf*. No questions about the ships we sunk, or the escapes we had. We would talk about ourselves and about Spike, and about the home we intended to build after the war.

That house had been started one quiet night in the sound shack when I was writing a letter to Marjorie. I talked about a house—a dream house. I even included a few sketches. In the next batch of mail, Marjorie included a number of suggestions. She had ideas about the location of the kitchen. Spike's room should be here. We'd have a sunroom there. Throughout the long months at sea in every letter I wrote I carried the plans a bit further. Finally between us, we had it finished, just as we wanted it. The last time I saw Spike he was twenty-six days old. I wondered about my brother Roy. He owns a bar in 'Frisco. I promised myself a terrific binge there. Angela, his wife, would top off the evening with her specialty—a spaghetti dinner with all the trimmings. Toward dawn I fell asleep, and it seemed only a few minutes before Lamby was shaking me, telling me it was time for my watch.

We arrived at the new patrol area in midafternoon, and things began to pop at once. It began when Lieutenant Mercer, at the periscope, summoned the Captain. He had spotted a ship—a two-mast affair.

"You're right," observed Captain Warder. "Here are the masts, now ... Battle stations!"

Our approach was perfect. We fired a few moments later, and the whine of the fish heading straight for the Jap was music in my ears. This time there was no miss. I began to report it.

"They're going ..." I wasn't able to complete the sentence. A terrific explosion rocked the *Wolf.* It was the concussion from our torpedo; we must have struck a munitions carrier. It was as terrific and deafening as a depth charge. I tore off the earphones and held my splitting head. My ears were ringing. Maley was shouting, but I couldn't make out his words. He pointed to the intercom system. I leaned over and pressed my ear against it and heard the Captain giving a blow-by-blow description of the sinking ship. His voice sounded as if he were at the end of a bad telephone connection.

"Christ, boys," he was yelling. "We knocked the lifeboats right off her ... There go the smokestacks ... Some damn fool is trying to blow the whistle, steam is coming out of there. There go the Nips jumping over like rats. There's a second explosion. She's going down already. She's breaking apart." He paused and called to Lieutenant Mercer: "Jim, hurry up if you want a picture of this. Only the stern is showing now."

Ensign Mercer clipped his camera to the eyepiece. "Got her, sir," he said.

A moment later Captain Warder, back at the periscope, announced, "There she goes ... Good-by!"

My ears still rang from the first blast, but I replaced my phones and listened. A few minutes later I heard the underseas roar that meant her boilers had exploded.

Paul took off his headset. He leaned over and yelled in my ear.

"That's one Jap bastard that won't do any damage, Eck!"

The Captain, still scanning the surface, kept up a running description. I put my ear against the intercom again.

"Congratulations, forward room and sound," he was saying. "Good work, everybody. Wait a minute: There are lifeboats up there. Men are swarming over the sides. Damn it, this sinking can be seen from the beach very easily. I can't take any chances. We'll have to take prisoners rather than let them hit the beach and spread the alarm."

126

His voice dropped. "I don't understand that ... Wait a minute, though ... Yes, I do! We blew the oars right out of the boat. I've been wondering why they weren't rowing. There must have been plenty of men on that ship ... I'm figuring on going into that Gulf, and I don't want those men to spread the alarm. We'll track them until dark. If conditions permit, we'll take prisoners." He kept his eye to the periscope. Men were swimming aimlessly about; others were clinging to spars and debris. Every piece of wreckage had a figure clinging to it. "Those lifeboats are crowded to the rims now," he went on. "There's a lot of people swimming around up there yet. All right Jim, mark this lifeboat, zero ... zero ... five ... Look out for signs of activity. Let me know at once if anything shows up."

He turned the periscope over to Ensign Mercer. As he came by the sound shack, he looked in. "Good work, boys," he said. "Take it easy for a little while. We may be busy later."

Lieutenant Deragon went over our records to see if we could identify the ship we'd sunk.

A few minutes later Ensign Mercer, after checking tides and currents, told the Captain the Japs were being floated out toward the Celebes. They were on their way to the open sea, without oars or provisions. According to the charts, the nearest land was 600 miles to the south.

Captain Warder was silent for a moment. "Well," he said at last, "we won't have any prisoners tonight." He paused again. "They'll never make it. Those poor bastards swimming around ... Well, there's nothing we can do about them."

We waited until darkness and then surfaced. Jap lifeboats were still bobbing up and down. They must have been a terrified group when they saw the long black shape of the *Seawolf* bear down on them. The first two Japanese the Captain saw were youngsters. They looked about sixteen, he said. They were stark naked, clinging to two pieces of wreckage. Their clothes had been blown off by the blast. The Captain leaned over the rail cable. "Savvy English?" he shouted.

One boy turned, screamed what sounded like a panic-stricken warning, then let go of his piece of wreckage and swam off. The Captain shouted after him, but he churned the water like a long-distance swimmer and finally vanished in the darkness. Captain Warder asked the remaining boy if he could "Savvy English." The other shook his head.

"Sousa," the Captain called, "go down to the rail and see if you can make out a name on that wreckage."

Eddie leaned far over and examined several pieces floating about, but he could find no identification.

Sousa threw a line out to the boy, but the Jap chattered and would have nothing to do with it. Sousa shouted in exasperation, "Grab hold the line, grab hold!" but the Jap pushed it away each time it dropped nearby. Captain Warder watched this scene silently.

"All right, Sousa, you can't do anything with him," he said finally. "Pass the word below to bring up a life jacket and a bottle of whisky." They were handed up and tossed to the Jap. He caught them and held them. Captain Warder commented dryly:

"If he puts on that jacket and drinks the whisky, he'll never know what hit him."

The current was strong. In a few minutes the Jap who wouldn't be rescued was out of sight and on his way to the open sea.

At that he was given more than the men on the *Perch*, and the *Sea Lion*, and the *Shark*. They didn't even get a life jacket or a bottle of whisky.

We were on the double alert all night. When you sink a ship and then return to the same area, you're inviting trouble. The Skipper decided to patrol outside the harbor for a period of watchful waiting. We were on the alert, too, for mine fields. We saw hostile aircraft and ignored them. After surfacing that night the Captain decided to go into the Gulf again. We sneaked into the Gulf before diving, and at this point we were less than twenty miles from a beehive of Jap activity. We pushed on silently, nearer and nearer to the Jap center. We upped a cautious periscope.

"I can see a church steeple, some houses," the Skipper reported. "Looks like a lot of shipping in there. I see several masts ... Can't go in there, boys, that's mined. Let's take a look over here.... *Hmmmm,* could be at that ... What a wonderful camouflage job ... Left full rudder, Rudy ... I think there's a ship over there, but I'm not sure. If it is, it's a big one. Battle stations! Sure that's a ship ... She's a beauty ... Motor ship, with a cruiser stern ... Heavy guns aft ... looks brand new to me ... What a camouflage job! ... I can see them loading her, probably hemp. This ship is tied up to a wharf or anchored right off one. She's a beauty. This should be an easy attack if we can avoid detection. Down periscope."

Silence. Then: "What course are we steering, Jim? Where are we? Let me have a look here. This is a ticklish spot to get out of in case they send somebody out here looking for us, as I expect them to ... So that's where we are ... Well, I want to work up to this point and take a zero angle shot. How about the tides and the current drift?"

Captain Warder was thorough as usual. We worked our way slowly in. The water was shallow, but the possibility of mines kept us even more tense. This place surely must have a mine field.

I could almost sense Maley's thoughts. Again, up periscope.

"Just as I thought," observed the Skipper. "Down periscope. Make ready the bow tubes. Sound, I won't need you on this attack, but I want you to track these fish. I want to know especially if any of them run erratic ... Bow tubes ready? O.K., open the outer doors. Rudy, this is going to be ticklish, and I'm going to have to coach you on. Up periscope. We will fire this time if everything is the same up here."

The periscope hit its upper level, and the Captain was on it like a leech.

"Okay, they haven't seen us. They're loading hemp, all right. Boy, she's a beauty! Henry, I'm going to fire. Are you ready? ... Rudy, come left more, come left a hair, steady, hold her steady ... Fire! ... Eckberg, are they running?"

"They're running, Captain—hot and straight."

"Yes, I see 'em now, number two is going to miss, number three is going to hit."

Boom! I heard her go. What an explosion!

The whole ship seethed with excitement.

Captain Warder watched intently. "She's listing heavily to port. Seems to be settling heavily. The guns are manned and firing wildly—in all directions. They don't know what hit them. We must have caught them flat-footed ... Now, what is this? ... Boy, what damage control they must have! They have righted the ship and taken off the list ... Oh, no, my friends! ... Not that easy! ... Make ready the aftertubes ... Rudy, swing her around!"

The *Wolf* swung completely around, attacked again—from the stern. More of our torpedoes crashed into her. Captain Warder waited impatiently until the smoke cleared away.

"We blew their aft guns to bits. The forward gun is manned, but the crew is standing there. They're probably dazed. Wait, there's a fire breaking out in the bow. They're abandoning ship ... There she goes settling in the water. Wait a minute! What have we here? Here come some Zeros! They're peppering my periscope."

We heard the *rat-tat-tat* of the machine guns. But Captain Warder was determined to see this large Jap vessel sink, Zeros or no Zeros.

"Dammit," he exploded, "that ship must be honeycombed with watertight compartments. It won't do any good to put any more fish into her now, unless I can place it ... *Hmmmm.* Damn those planes! Damn them! Well, I'm going to throw one more at her and see what happens. Up periscope. Rudy, come right, now. Steady. Are you ready, Hank? Okay—Fire!" Pause. "Well, there she goes, boys. She's going up in smoke. Fires are breaking out all over her. I believe she's sitting on the bottom in very shallow water. Come on, I'm satisfied. Take a couple of snaps, Jim, and then let's get the hell out of here."

I heard the sound of many screws. The anti-sub boats were still hunting for us. I gave the Captain their bearings.

"We'll have to get out of here," he said.

The Japs were coming closer, throwing depth charges right and left. They were missing completely. The *Wolf* headed out for the mouth of the Gulf. We had to get out of here fast. We knew the Japs would immediately take protective measures. It would be suicide to stay.

It was now late afternoon. We raced under a flat sea, with a bright sun in the sky. It was risky periscope weather. Seventy miles should take us—Just then the

Captain's voice broke in. "Oh, here's another one. Looks like—yes, it is a big Maru ... We'll take her. Sound, this will have to be your approach."

I heard the freighter zigzagging, seeking frantically to escape. She knew we were stalking her. This Maru was doing about 120 degrees zigs. I told the Captain, and he called back:

"Eckberg, I'm getting ready to fire. She should be on the port bow now. Got her?"

The Captain upped the periscope and took a look. He said, "Oh, Christ! Down periscope! Take 'er deep!"

We went down fast. I heard the screws of this Maru coming at us. Then she was over us. It was like standing under a trestle while a freight train rumbled overhead. She was still zigzagging and had no idea where we were.

The Captain again put the *Seawolf* on the course to the Gulf's mouth. He left the conning tower and went to his room. For the next four hours I listened intently for the freighter, but she was gone. The *Wolf* was moving south at a rapid pace. My eyes were tired. I took off the earphones. Maley was absent-mindedly doodling on a scratch pad.

"I'm going to hit the sack," I told him.

He nodded. "O.K., Eck."

Lamberson was asleep in his bunk next to mine. He woke up as I got in. "Where the hell are we, Eck?" he asked drowsily.

"On the way out of this damn gulf," I told him.

He yawned loudly and turned on his other side. "I don't want to be on the next sub that pokes her nose into this gulf," he said. Then, after a minute, he sat up restlessly and began rubbing his eyes. "Guess I'll play a little solitaire."

He climbed down, got a deck of cards, and sat on an overturned water bucket. He used a chair for a table.

"Hope we go east, Eck," he said. "That means home, and will I be glad to see it!"

I had closed my eyes, trying to force myself to sleep. My nerves were still tingling from the long stretch I had just completed.

I fell into uneasy sleep. It seemed as if I had closed my eyes for only a few minutes when the alarm went. When I hit the deck seven feet below my bunk, it jarred me awake. I raced up the three steps through the watertight hatch to the officers' quarters, squirmed down the narrow passageway. It was like a subway rush. Crew members were pushing each other along. I had to buck this human tide. Finally I reached the after end of the forward battery, then the control room. There wasn't any talking. Each man had a job to do and we didn't waste time in talking. I took over sound.

The Captain's voice broke the silence. "This ship has something on the forward deck that I can't make out. He apparently doesn't see us, he's not zigging at all. This will be a big day if we can get him. Sound, can we pick him up yet?"

I said: "Yes, Captain, I have him now."

"Very well!" said the Captain. "This is a 5,000- to 7,000-ton freighter, two goal posts, stack amidships, looks like coal-burner, estimated speed nine knots, course, three five zero. The decks are loaded with what looks like invasion barges... The crew is in white uniforms, well disciplined. This is probably a Jap naval reserve ship. We'll plunk him."

I gave sound bearings, and in a few minutes the approach party gave him the bearings for firing. "All right, Willie," he said, "stand by to fire. Ready, Henry?" Bringelman was at the Captain's right shoulder with his hands on the solenoid controls ready to push the firing buttons. Henry answered: "All set, Captain."

Then the order came, "Fire!"

I caught the fish as they left the *Wolf*, The Captain said, "I can see them. One's going to hit ...!" I heard the terrific blast.

"There's no running around," the Skipper said. "They don't seem to be panicky. Everybody seems to have a destination. She's listing to starboard. There's a group of them forward, trying to clear the invasion barges, trying to save them. They won't have time. They are going to go too fast. Yes, they have abandoned the idea. These people are cool, calm, and collected. Right now they are throwing everything that will float over the side. There's no time to launch any lifeboats."

I interrupted. "Ship coming up the starboard quarter, sir." Her laboring screws sounded like a minesweeper.

"O.K., Eck, we'll have a look," the Captain said. "Hell, it's those anti-sub vessels again. Converted minesweepers." He paused. "Is that all they can get out here?" he asked. "That's an insult to my ship and crew."

There was a distant boom: the Jap was clumsily dropping depth charges.

We went deep. I could hear the ship breaking up, and finally her boilers exploded.

We stayed down the rest of that day. Everybody was exhausted. The torpedomen, who had been reloading and reloading, were asleep on their feet. Gus Wright had made sandwiches all day long. He was carrying coffee to me every half-hour or so.

We surfaced that night with normal routine. We were still in the Gulf. Again I slept badly. The day's excitement was too much. I woke about 3 a.m. Swede was on watch in the control room.

"What are you doing up, Eck?" he asked.

"Not sleepy, I guess," I said, and downed some of his coffee.

"Sleepy, hell," he said. "What's worrying you is worrying me and everybody on this boat. We are inside the Gulf, that's all, and we'll feel better when we get way outside." He was right.

It could not have been three minutes later that Franz yelled from the conning tower: "Stand by to dive!"

Swede jumped to his controls. For a huge man, he was as quick as a cat. I took off for the sound room. I couldn't find a thing.

Ensign Casler was the officer of the deck, and had picked up a smell of smoke. He couldn't see anything, but didn't take a chance and ordered a crash dive. Diving and cruising submerged upset our schedule, since we couldn't make the speed submerged that we could on the surface. We'd hoped to reach the entrance by dawn, then submerge. But it was only an hour until daylight now, and so we continued submerged. About an hour after my morning watch was over, I was back in the engine room, playing my favorite Froggy Bottom record.

Suddenly there was the cry of "Battle Stations." I grabbed at the machine to stop it and shattered the record. I ran to the sound room ready to kill every Jap in Japan. My favorite record lying in a thousand pieces! I got in the sound shack.

"Another target," Paul said. "Too damn far away to tell what it is."

Captain Warder had his periscope up. "Well, boy," he said, "I rather wish we weren't on a time schedule. This is like a picnic. I can't tell yet, but this looks like an old freighter. Might not be worth a fish."

Then I caught her screws. She was a coal-burning freighter, making slow speed.

A few minutes later Captain Warder caught sight of her. "She's not so small, at that. About four thousand tons. Loaded to the gunwales. We'll plunk this baby, too."

We went in for the kill. I caught the screws of anti-sub vessels again. They were about three to five miles away. We came to the firing point. "Fire!" I heard the dull thud of the first explosion.

"We really cracked her this time, men. I can't see anything for smoke," came the Captain's voice.

We headed out toward the open sea. We moved out of the Gulf and could relax at last.

I grabbed a nap that afternoon. Then I went back in the sound shack working on "Begin the Beguine." I must have been loud.

Zerk stuck his head out of the after-battery hatch.

"For Christ sake, knock off the goddamn noise, damn it!" he yelled.

I yelled back: "Go on back in your hole, you ant-faced baboon!"

Before I knew it the whole battery was shouting, "Shut up, can it, keep it quiet." They accused Zerk of making noise. I kept quiet. Zerk explained hotly that he was only telling me to keep quiet. "I wasn't making the noise, it was Eckberg!" He came out into the passageway. They shouted him down. "Shut up, damn it, Zerk." He went back mumbling.

I started copying code, and after about half an hour I realized we were headed in an easterly course. It suddenly dawned on me: home was in that direction. I got so excited I left my station for the first time in my navy career and rushed out into the control room. The first man I saw was Lieutenant Deragon.

"Where are we going, Mr. Deragon?" I asked him.

"You're overdue, Eck," he said with a grin. "I knew as soon as we changed course you'd be out here. We expect to go home. How's that?"

That was all right with me. At last we were headed home. We still had Palau to go by, and that was tough, but we were headed home.

The next three days were uneventful. We spotted nothing.

Near dusk of the fourth day, the periscope officer picked up an island. We closed in to run a patrol in front of it. Conditions were in our favor. We had a nice chop, it was a cloudy day, and just enough rain was falling to make our periscope almost invisible to the enemy and yet permit us to look around.

We moved in carefully and spotted a patrol boat. He was too far away to be dangerous. Captain Warder, scanning with the utmost care, picked up the masts of a ship coming in our general direction. The Jap—it turned out to be a destroyer—was making tremendous speed. The Skipper sounded battle stations. But as we maneuvered, we realized that from her speed and the angle on our bow it would be impossible to launch an attack. The weather conditions had turned bad. The rain, which had aided us at first, now poured down in sheets, making our visibility almost nil. We were in the midst of a typical tropical squall. The Captain peered through and saw two more destroyers come charging by.

"Well, we have to let that first baby go by," he said ... "But these two— What in the hell is their hurry? Maybe they are heading for the Gulf, to clean us out of there. I think I'm going to tackle this one." He studied the sea. "This will be a terrific shot if I can make it," he said, almost under his breath. "He's really making speed." He ordered: "All ahead, full right rudder. We have to go like hell to get this fellow."

The *Wolf* quivered with the speed. We veered to our left to get into position. We were on this course for about five minutes, the Skipper taking sweeps with his periscope, when he exclaimed:

"Well, I'll be goddamned! At my age, too! To think I would fall for a trick like that! Here is an aircraft carrier, and I'm out of position! I've been sucked in by this goddamned destroyer, and now it's impossible to make the attack. Look at that big beautiful bastard! She's really spinning! Looks new to me. The length of that flight deck looks to be about six hundred feet." I think he could have bawled. None of us believe that the Captain was at fault. We had been closing to run our patrol, and it wasn't his fault if the Jap ships chose this time to make their appearance. We were not out of position because we had not left our original course long enough to make any difference. Had we stayed on a course that would have brought us up to the patrol point, we still would have missed the carrier because she was traveling at such high speed. Captain Warder was too cagey to be sucked in by anyone.

We surfaced. It was near dusk. By this time the carrier was out of sight. It seemed apparent that the destroyers and the carrier were rushing to a rendezvous. Captain Warder wanted to find that rendezvous.

The Japs were probably meeting there preparing for an attack on the Solomons. We could be of damn good use if we walked in on them.

The *Wolf* was put on 100 percent power—to go as fast as she could. The speed indicator in the control room spun around like mad. It vibrated all the way up to a point that we hadn't seen in eight months. We swept that surrounding ocean like a broom.

Suddenly, as I sat in sound, I realized something had changed.

Something was missing. Then I had it. The high-pitched endless whine of our electric motors was gone. I peered into the control room. There were Captain Warder and Lieutenant Deragon, looking glumly at a chart.

"Hell," said the Skipper, disgusted, and vanished in the direction of his stateroom, Deragon with him.

I hurried out and looked at the chart. The *Wolf* had a new course laid out, taking her to Pearl Harbor. I went back to my shack, wondering what this all meant, and a moment later Captain Warder came in. His face was expressionless. He had a message to send. I turned the transmitter up and contacted an Allied Command.

Our message was brief. We had sighted the carrier. This was her course and her apparent destination. And something I had not known—the *Seawolf* was having serious electrical trouble. That's why we were going to Pearl Harbor. It was the main motor generator cables which had gone bad. They grew so hot we feared a fire. A bad fire in the batteries would cripple us. We'd be unable to dive. And in these Jap-infested waters, it would mean the finish for all of us.

By morning the electricians had fixed things well enough for us to resume our patrol. Captain Warder now set our course for another island. This was next on our schedule, and the Skipper felt the *Wolf* was in good enough shape to make it before going into Pearl Harbor for complete repairs. It was a small island boasting an airfield, bristling with gun emplacements. We reached it before dawn. Captain Warder studied the island through the periscope. "Nice beach here. Wouldn't mind going in for a swim," he commented. "This is a pretty little place. I see barracks, lots of them, on top of hills. I can see what looks like gun emplacements. I can see radio-antenna towers. There is a ship in the harbor. She's only a sailing vessel, though. This is a typical South Pacific island."

We spent several days hunting for trouble. No luck. Then, finally, we set an easterly course for Pearl Harbor. On the way Captain Warder spotted ships. The *Wolf* prepared to attack—an attack that was to prove one of the most dangerous she ever tried.

"Seems to be a whole mess of ships," the Skipper said. "This one Maru looks big enough. We'll plunk him ... Wait a minute. Of all things to blunder into! Look what we got this time!"

We had a pretty good idea down in sound. Maley and I had a number of sets of screws going in our ears.

"We've got screws all over this damn place," I called to the Skipper.

"I'm not surprised, Eck," he said, a little ruefully. "We're barged into a floating cannery and her brood of fishing boats."

Fishing boats! And thick as flies! That was bad. Fishing boats meant deep, heavy nets hanging down; and if our propellers struck a net, we'd have to surface—in the face of gun batteries that could blast us out of the water.

"Well, see if you can get me a range." Captain Warder's words were easy.

I tried. There were too many ships.

"Make ready the bow tubes," came a moment later. "This will be a difficult attack. ..." A few minutes went by ... "Fire one! Damn it, we missed! ... Damn that bastard!"

We dove deep. On sound I heard the ship and her brood scuttling away. She dropped two depth charges as a parting salute, but they were mild.

The next day we sighted two more ships, one heading south, one north. They were not alone. Jap bombers roared overhead, and patrol vessels played sentry on either side. The *Wolf* tried for the ships anyway. They were racing along at twenty-five knots or better. We could not close the range sufficiently to launch an attack. We gave it up, finally, knowing we had not been detected, and pushed on for Pearl.

We were less than five days out of Pearl when the shout came, "Plane above the port bow!"

We stood by to dive.

"We don't have to dive for that baby," came a moment later. "It's a PBY."

We felt like cheering below. We were in home waters now. We wanted to be topside, and we wanted to be up there badly.

For many weeks I hadn't seen sunlight or tasted fresh air. I must have looked the way I felt. "Like a dirty turkish towel," was how Maley put it. I knew I had lost weight. My pants hung so loosely. I had to use new holes in my belt to keep them up. But we tried to forget about topside and set to work cleaning up the *Wolf.* Our cruise had been a real success. Pearl was the nearest to home we had been in two years. We worked and thought of home again. Family photographs suddenly came to light once more. We reread old letters.

In the mess hall one night I was talking to Rudy Gervais. He was in love with a girl in Connecticut. He had a curious sensation of being far too old for her—suddenly. She was young; he felt old as the hills.

"The last time I saw her I was just a kid," he complained. "Now I'm not a kid any more. She still is. How are we going to hit it off?"

"Aw, you're still a kid," I told him. "Don't worry, she'll be more than glad to have you."

"I don't know," he said. I looked at him. Shave off that beard, and he still would be taken for eighteen.

The eve of hitting Pearl, some of us below went up on the bridge. A handful of us went up at a time. When I came up, there were three figures standing by the rail. One was Lieutenant Syverson.

"Good evening, Eck," he said. "Come on up."

Then we stood there silently. No one spoke. We couldn't see the land. Moonlight shimmered on the water. It was a perfect night. The *Wolf* left a sparkling phosphorescent trail. It was a damn pretty thing to see. We all breathed deeply, and then, one by one, went below.

It was November, almost a year since the Jap attack. We had been out at sea nearly twelve months.

We sat around in a circle in Kelly's Pool Room that night, and we talked about Pearl. It was just 2,200 miles from home. I looked around at the men. We weren't the same men who had left Cavite a year ago. Sully had flicks of gray in his beard. Deep lines were etched in Maley's face. I had lost a lot of weight. Hank Brengelman's Santa Claus face wasn't roly-poly any more. Only Pop Rosario looked the same. He might have been thirty and he might have been fifty.

We talked about Pearl Harbor. How would she look? I remembered when I first saw it in 1929. There were only nine buildings and a couple of piers.

Sully exclaimed: "Damn it, Eck, there couldn't have been."

That started an argument that lasted for hours. Finally, about 2 A.M., I went to bed.

We had early reveille and were met by a destroyer escort to take us in. The order from the bridge was one we hadn't heard for a long time: "Station the channel watch." We were in Pearl.

Every few minutes somebody would yell: "Christ Almighty, look at that!" or "Look at those guns!"

The word finally came, "Secure the radio watch." Then: "If you are in the uniform of the day, come on deck."

This meant clean dungarees, shorts, shirts, and white hat. I had been prepared for this hours ago. I climbed topside, emerged from the conning tower, and stood transfixed. I was stunned by the sight and sound.

The *Seawolf* was slowly gliding into Pearl Harbor. But what a different spectacle than when we had last been here two years ago! It was unbelievable. The sky above us was darkened by huge, sausage-like barrage balloons. The harbor on both sides of us was a staggering scene of destruction, as though a tornado had twisted across it, overturning ships, snapping crane booms like matchsticks, splitting buildings in half. We passed piled-up fragments of planes, their wings jutting out grotesquely; ships splotched with huge holes, keels and hulls of nameless vessels. There was the screeching of moving derricks, the scream of air hammers, a bedlam of engines roaring, machines pounding, men at work.

The *Seawolf* moved slowly past a gigantic overturned hulk. Against its immensity, the men swarming over it appeared no larger than ants. Somebody on deck murmured in an awed voice: "The *Oklahoma!*" and I stared at it. To our right as we moved into dock lay a light cruiser with a damaged superstructure; on the left, we were passing Ford Island. It looked as though a hurricane had wrecked it. Trees were splintered, structures leveled to the ground. Directly ahead of us now was the submarine base. I had never seen so many submarines tied up before. Anti-aircraft guns bristled from every roof overlooking the harbor; sandbags were piled high in front of every building.

You could be sure of this: history would never record a second surprise attack on Pearl Harbor.

Quite a crowd waited on the dock to welcome us. I saw faces I hadn't seen for months. There were shouts of, "Hello, Skipper, how was the trip?" and "Good hunting, Captain?"

We tied up. Lieutenant Deragon made an announcement to the crew. "We are now in Pearl Harbor," he said formally. "The Captain expects to fuel up, take on supplies, and leave here the first possible moment. There will be free beer for the entire crew with the exception of the duty section."

We cheered that.

Lieutenant Deragon went on: "The beer is at the swimming pool. You men know where that is. You owe a vote of thanks for it to Commander Stephens, executive officer of the submarine base."

Captain Warder, smartly dressed in a new khaki uniform, as trim a naval officer as ever stepped on a deck, appeared from below.

Deragon concluded: "Now what we have done on this last patrol and where we have been is no one's business but our own. You men are free now. Go ashore and enjoy yourself. But be ready to leave at half an hour's notice. Now, I think Captain Warder has a few things he'd like to say."

Captain Warder stepped forward. He was all smiles. "Boys," he said, "this might sound repetitious. The only excuse I make for it is that I am sincere. I am proud of you all. We have made a fine record. We have a wonderful ship. To my way of thinking, we have the best submarine crew in the United States Navy. My thanks goes out to every one of you."

We stood there listening, and we liked it.

"I am now on my way to Admiral Nimitz's headquarters," he said. "If we can possibly do it, we will leave tomorrow. I know you are eager to get home, and so am I. Now, have a good time. I'll see you all up at the swimming pool."

We found ice-cold beer at the pool. The crew of the *Seawolf* relaxed. We lolled about, lying on the grass, taking it easy on the deck chairs, and letting the sun and air get at us. Captain Warder appeared an hour later, sank into a deck chair, and paid his acknowledgments to a glass of cold beer. A few minutes later Commander Stephens joined him.

Old Pop Mocarsky, who hadn't smiled in a year, marched up and stood in front of the Captain. He turned to the crew.

"How's the beer, boys?" Old Pop shouted. "O.K.?"

"O.K.! Pop," we shouted back. Captain Warder rose to his feet, put a hand on Pop's shoulder, and looked at all of us.

"Pop," he said, "the beer is fine. I'm fine, and you look fine. Today the whole world's fine."

After the party a group of us looked in at the ship's service store. There we saw the first American girl we'd seen in nearly two years. She was standing behind the counter, sorting handkerchiefs, and she was small and blonde, and pretty. She came up to wait on us. We stared at her. A red flush crept into her cheeks.

"What are you men looking at?" she said finally, trying to fight off a smile. "Do you want to buy something or not?"

We realized then that we must have looked pretty odd, with our beards, our cut-off dungarees, wearing no socks, and staring at her like high-school kids.

Sousa said, "Now, honey, you ought to feel honored. Got any socks?"

She had some, and we all solemnly bought ourselves one pair each.

We were like housewives on a shopping tour, going from counter to counter, looking at things, feeling them, smelling them.

Yet the ship was on our minds. We felt a little lost away from her. And all at once we got stage fright. We felt conspicuous. We wanted to get away from the lights and people's eyes, and down inside the *Wolf* again where lights were low and the faces around us, before and behind us, were the faces we knew. We hurried back. On the way we passed an officer. We had taken about four steps when he called out:

"Just a minute, sailors!"

We turned and stared at him.

"You failed to salute," he said.

For the first time in months we realized we were back in the Navy. We hadn't saluted an officer for a long, long time. Someone mumbled, "Sorry, sir," and we saluted and hurried on.

The *Wolf* was fueling up at the dock. Supplies were coming aboard. The entire crew was there. We had liberty, no one had called us back, and yet none of us felt comfortable more than a hundred yards away from the *Wolf*. We were going home. We weren't taking any chances.

Most of us sat up on deck that night and talked about home. I hit the sack early in the morning. Some of the others stayed topside and talked all through the night. I didn't sleep well. I was so accustomed to pitching and rolling that the lack of motion disturbed me.

At 4 p.m. the next afternoon the cry echoed: "All hands to quarters."

Sousa mustered the crew in three minutes flat. Not a man was missing.

"Stations for getting under way!" the order came.

I turned for a last look at Pearl Harbor, then I climbed down into the ship. The lines were pulled in; the sharp *rat-tat-tat* of our engines echoed across the harbor; we were escorted out by a destroyer; and after darkness fell, we set a straight course for San Francisco. We were heading home.

CHAPTER XI

The *Wolf* Comes Home

THE LAST trip of the *Wolf* was a rollicking one. Card games were in full swing in Kelly's Pool Room, and bull sessions went on at all hours. The Skipper dropped into the radio shack the second night.

"Eckberg, you're due for a little rest in the States," he said. "To insure that rest, is there any school you'd like to attend?"

I thought that over. If I knew anything, it was physics, and physics and electronics were becoming more and more important. Whole new worlds were opening up. "I'd like to brush up on radio, sir," I said.

He nodded. "Good!" he said. "Radio it is."

In much the same fashion Captain Warder made the rounds of all the old-timers, telling them they were due for a rest. The word had gone around that he was due for another war assignment. It would take him off the *Wolf.*

The trip was routine, but cold. As we came farther north, we began to freeze. We'd been in tropical waters for a long time. We'd lived in a pair of shorts and little else for months. Bit by bit we began to pile covering on us. Pretty soon I was wearing an old leather jacket, and under that two sweatshirts, then a dungaree shirt, and then an undershirt. In my bunk I shivered under two woolen blankets. Loaiza was muttering constantly about the "frigid" weather, lamenting in Spanish, "I can't stand it another minute."

We were about halfway home when we began discussing our perennial question, what were we going to do our first night home. I knew what I'd do. First I'd telephone Marjorie. I'd talk to Spike over the telephone. He might even be able to say, "Hello, Pop." I'd get a kick out of that. Then I'd drop over and surprise my brother Roy in his barroom.

About midnight some of the crew began to drift into the radio room. The shack normally held three men, if they weren't too big, but before long six were in it somehow. How the bull flew! Every man was determined that the rest of the gang had to hear what he was going to do. We were given graphic descriptions, long and detailed. But after a while the men began to drift out. We were all impatient. None of us could stay in one place long. For the first time the *Wolf* was beginning to cramp us. We were focusing on the world outside, and that world was terribly big. Only Maley and I were left, and idly I brought out our old song book. There it was, little the worse for wear. And there was the song, "Begin the Beguine." The book fell open to the page. I mused over the words. I thought, *How many times I've opened this old book to that page and these words diverted my mind from things that wouldn't let me relax.* "Begin the

Beguine," whether I knew the words or not, was an old friend of mine. And pretty soon I was humming it, and Maley joined me, and we were both singing at the top of our lungs. We were happy. Nobody complained, but now and then an alarmed head was stuck in. The *Wolf*'s crew was relaxed. Not so long ago one peep out of us, and protests rained about our heads. We'd been under tension. Everybody had been living on nerve—all save Captain Warder, I think. Somehow he knew the secret of relaxation.

In my own case the tension of these last twelve months was to stay with me for a long time after I came home. Marjorie was to be unhappy, Spike afraid to talk to me, because I was so irritable. For weeks after, I'd wake up at two and three in the morning, walk around, smoke half a dozen cigarettes, and try to fall asleep again. For a long time I couldn't sleep more than three hours at a time.

We were still singing when Lieutenant Deragon poked his head around the corner. We shut up. We must have been pretty loud to bother him. He came into the doorway a minute later, arms akimbo, looked at us, and finally announced:

"Eckberg, I have listened to you moan and groan that damn thing for about a year now. That in itself is all right, but every time you tackle it, it becomes worse. Now either learn the words or shut up."

I'd already shut up, so I just grinned at him.

The *Wolf* moved on. The night of the fifth day out, I strolled into Kelly's Pool Room. Dishman, Zerk, Swede, and a few other men were in there, with John Street the center of attention. They had been discussing the *Wolf*'s toll of Jap ships. John was sitting there, chewing on a pencil, a pad of paper in front of him. "O.K.," he was saying, "here's the way I figure it." I sat in. I'd heard a hell of a lot of those ships go down. He was adding the totals. "Comes out to over a dozen ships known sunk, and maybe half a dozen damaged. That's not bad."

"Not bad!" I said. "Hell, it's wonderful."

"You want to remember," Dishman put in, "most of these we got were men-of-war. The *Wolf* did okay. There's nobody got anything to say against her."

The *Wolf* came in sight of the Golden Gate. The word came down from the bridge and ran through the ship like wildfire. Requests to go topside were flying up to the conning tower. The reply came, "Nobody allowed on the bridge." It seems we had a rendezvous with a ship which was to escort us into the Gate. As soon as we passed the Gate, deck hatches were opened.

"Let the boys up on deck," said the Skipper, "but pass the word that it is cold up here, and they'd better put on all the clothes they have."

There was a mad rush to the hatches. We were making good speed, and when I came up, the wind almost took my breath away. And the cold. The wind whistled down the deck with numbing effect. The first thing I saw was the mountainous Golden Gate. It looked somber under a dreary gray sky. I could see the pencil-white line of surf, and in the distance, the outline of familiar sights. My mind was in a whirl. Here was the good old U.S.A.! God, I was glad to see it! I stood there and stared. Here was home. Here was a place I hadn't seen for twenty-five long months. I thought, *What in hell ever made the Japs think they could overrun my home?* Why, every man, woman, and child would have used clubs to keep them away if they had to. The Japs might have caught us by surprise at Pearl Harbor, but this was home. No Jap would ever dare to try anything here. I don't think I ever had such sense of pride and love for my country as I had on the deck of the *Wolf* that cold day, cruising slowly over the slate-black waters into port.

Suddenly we stopped. I thought, *What now?* In peacetime we could expect to be held up by customs officials and agents of the Department of Agriculture. If one of these inquisitive fellows was coming aboard, I'd gladly volunteer to throw him into the bay. We certainly had no agricultural produce on the *Wolf.* We didn't have enough fresh fruit to feed an ant. A speedboat dashed out to us. A young Navy lieutenant clambered aboard. We must have looked bedraggled and woebegone compared to this pink-cheeked young officer. We were bundled up in sweaters, our underwear was hanging out of our shorts, we were unshaven, our noses were red, our cheeks sunken, and we had six- to nine-inch beards. What was this stranger aboard for? "Why, he's the pilot," somebody said. A pilot? We resented that. Our Skipper managed to bring us through all sorts of hell without a pilot, didn't he? He could bring the *Wolf* in here with his eyes closed. In a few minutes we got under way again. The air was full of planes now. It seemed strange to stand on deck and not hear the order, "Take her down." Subconsciously we expected to be strafed any minute. We proceeded up that bay, and now it seemed the entire water front was celebrating our arrival. Whistles were blowing, flags were flying, and overhead the planes were dipping in salute. For us? I couldn't get it. None of us on deck could. Why, the *Wolf,* so far as the man on the street was concerned, was a ghost. She was a submarine that had been commissioned one December day, before the war, and then vanished, except for a brief note here and there. All anyone knew was that the *Seawolf* had done herself proud. How did that Navy announcement read? ... "a cruise that would go down as one of the epic stories of submarine warfare"?

Then we woke up. A battered cruiser was coming into harbor at the same time. We stared at her. Somebody said, "Hell, that's who they're welcoming, not us." We felt a little silly, and a little hurt, too. Didn't anyone know we were coming in, too?

At first we didn't recognize the Navy Yard. It seemed expanded to four times its size. We steamed past all sizes and shapes of ships we'd never seen before. We stared at one ship that was the craziest-looking vessel we'd ever seen.

"What's that, a garbage lighter?" someone asked.

"It's a scow," somebody else said.

Then the word was passed along: "It's one of those invasion barges." We were mortified to think we didn't know what an invasion barge looked like.

"Don't you guys know there's a war on?" someone cracked.

The *Wolf* finally neared the sub dock. She glided in. We were home.

Now Deragon stepped out in front of the crew. "Boys," he said, "I'm working to get leave parties arranged. All rate thirty days' furlough. We expect to be here from two and a half to three months. Half of the crew goes first, then the other half." He stopped. "The rest of the time," he said, "we'll work like fools getting the *Wolf* back to sea."

I was frantic to get to a phone to call Marjorie. She hadn't heard from me since our last stop in Australia more than two months before. Finally I was able to dash across the gangplank and touch the earth of the States again. I got on my knees and kissed the ground. I thought I was alone in the darkness, but a woman saw me and giggled.

I ran a half-mile to the barracks and didn't stop until I came to a telephone booth. Half the *Wolf*'s duty section was there.

They were all supposed to be on board; but, like me, they couldn't wait to get in touch with their families.

I went over to the Navy Yard canteen and got $10 worth of change, nickels, dimes, and quarters. Then I sat in line for the telephone. Nobody said a word. I was fourth. I went into the booth. It was hot and smelled of cigarette smoke. I plunked my money on the board under the phone.

"Get me Chicago," I told the long-distance operator.

"I'm sorry," her cool voice came back. "You will have to wait six hours."

"Six hours! Why?"

"There are important calls going on," she said.

"They can't be any more important than mine," I said. "I want to tell my wife I'm alive and back in the States."

She said: "Sorry, sir, but that is classified as a personal call."

I slammed the receiver down, picked up my money, and walked out. The others had the same experience. I walked away almost ready to bawl. Here I hadn't been home in two years. I hadn't heard my wife's voice in all that time. I hadn't seen my youngster. I was terribly homesick. Halfway back to the boat I decided to send Marjorie a wire. I turned on my heel and sent the wire from the same telephone booth.

Arrived West Coast port safely. Looks like I'm staying awhile. Grab an extra pair of pants and Spike, catch first train for 'Frisco. All love, Mel.

The next morning we went about town, and we were really introduced to a new United States. We stood and stared at lady welders, lady truck drivers, and wondered what in hell had happened to the country.

That afternoon a committee of the crew went out and bought a wristwatch and some luggage as a gift for the Skipper before we moved off the *Seawolf*.

When it came time for me to open my locker and take my personal belongings on shore, I knew I was saying good-by to the *Wolf*. It had been more than just a steel structure to me. I'd lived and died a thousand times on this ship. Men whom I admired more than any others I know, had lived and worked with me on this ship. I knew every bulkhead, every odor. She held no secrets from me. I walked through her before I took off my stuff, letting my mind wander over all the *Wolf* had done: the evacuations of men and matériel; the High Command, the aviators, ammunition, depth charges, Christmas Island—a thousand places, a thousand thrills. After dinner the word went through the ship, "All hands on the barge." Captain Warder came over the gangway. We stiffened to attention. He was wearing all his decorations, but he looked unhappy.

"Boys," he began, "you know it is a custom in submarines when the Captain is relieved for him to make a little farewell speech. It is something every skipper dreads. Well, I've come to say good-by. I have new orders. I am to be relieved. I'll be back out there before any of you. There is no use going into details about what I think of you."

He stopped. We saw tears rolling down his cheeks, and some of us were beginning to sniffle, too. "Sincerely, I have been very fortunate," he continued. "Here, I believe, is the best submarine crew ever gathered together. I know the man who is taking this ship out, and although many of you are leaving the *Wolf*, I want those of you who are remaining aboard to give him the same unswerving loyalty that you have given me. He is a good man, and he knows his submarines. Now I'm going to shake hands with every one of you and say, 'Good luck and a pleasant cruise.'"

There was a lump in my throat. My eyes smarted. I knew if I stayed there much longer I would start bawling. Then Sousa stepped out.

"Captain," he said, "we hate to see you go. Speaking for the men and myself, we have been very fortunate, too, having you for a captain. As you know, it is also a custom in submarines when a captain is being relieved and the crew does not like to see him go, to give him some token of their feelings. We would like to present you with this watch, which we had engraved coming from us, your crew, and this luggage which we thought you might need."

"Thank you," said Captain Warder, and his voice trembled.

"Thank you all, boys."

We lined up and shook hands. When he came to me, he said:

"Good-by, Eckberg, and good luck."

I managed to choke out, "Good-by, Captain, I hope I can serve with you again some day."

He gripped my hand hard. "Nothing would please me more, Eckberg," he said. He was escorted to the gangplank by Lieutenant Deragon. They shook hands, then Captain Warder slapped his executive officer's shoulder, turned, and waved to us. He walked over the gangplank to the dock and was gone.

He had brought his ship and his men safely home.

THE END

Made in the USA
Monee, IL
21 July 2021

74021476R00085